# CRAFTS OF THE WEIMAR BAUHAUS 1919–1924

# WEIMAR crafts of the bauhaus

## 1919–1924/AN EARLY EXPERIMENT IN INDUSTRIAL DESIGN
### BY WALTHER SCHEIDIG/PHOTOGRAPHS BY KLAUS G. BEYER

REINHOLD PUBLISHING CORPORATION, NEW YORK

Translated from the German by Ruth Michaelis-Jena with the collaboration of Patrick Murray, F.S.A. (Scot)

The original edition was published in 1966 by Edition Leipzig under the title: Bauhaus Weimar/Werkstattarbeiten. Copyright 1966 Edition Leipzig, 600/15/66. English language edition © 1967 Studio Vista Limited. Published in the United States of America 1967 by Reinhold Publishing Corporation, 430 Park Avenue, New York, N.Y. 10022. All rights reserved. Library of Congress Catalog Card No 66-25545. Printed in Germany by Fortschritt Erfurt  The following notice is printed in accordance with United States Customs regulations: bound in Great Britain. Printed in USSR occupied East Germany.

**T**he *Bauhaus* was an early experiment in bringing together the arts and crafts and academic art. It did much pioneering work in this field. It also tried to associate individuals with their differing ideas on creative work, without undue direction from above. Four years of the *Bauhaus* are a chapter in the history of art. They are also part of social history, reflecting as they do the fermenting human situation of a nation and a period.

Oskar Schlemmer, Diary June 1923

In May 1919, six months after the end of the First World War, students of the German art schools received an exciting pamphlet. "Architects, sculptors and painters, we must all return to the crafts. For art is not a profession. There is no essential difference between the artist and the craftsman... Let us create a new guild of craftsmen, without those class distinctions which raise an arrogant barrier between craftsmen and artists. Together let us conceive and create the new building of the future which will embrace architecture, sculpture and painting in unity and one day will rise to the skies, from the hands of millions of workers, as the crystal symbol of a new coming faith." On the front of this bright-yellow folder was a woodcut showing a cubist impression of a three-spired, three-naved Gothic cathedral. From the tops of the spires shone three five-pointed stars.

This manifesto, effective in expression and form, was Walter Gropius' publicity folder for the *Bauhaus* in Weimar. Its founding, principles and programme were announced, following the manifesto. Many of the young people who saw the pamphlet still wore field-grey. They had only recently escaped from the drill of military service and the inferno of the trenches. Now they were back at the same art schools where they had been students before call-up. They found it difficult to settle again in the studios and lecture rooms where – what seemed to them ages ago – they had been forced to put aside brush, chisel or ruler, to learn the use of hand-grenades and machine-guns. Many of them thought it senseless to start once more designing houses, painting landscapes or modelling from the nude, as the pre-war curriculum demanded. In opposition to this, Gropius' manifesto took account of the disturbing events of the last five years, and of the experiences of young people who had lived through them. Manifesto and woodcut hinted at many of the things that these young people had experienced even during the short interval of peace and their return to civilian life. Some of them would recognise the woodcut as a work of Lyonel Feininger, who belonged to the circle of the Berlin *Sturm*. In the *Sturm* Herwarth Walden had tried, since 1912, to draw attention to the implications of Italian futurism, French cubism, and Russian constructivism. Other young artists may have taken the Gothic church for an allusion to Catholicism. Also, they may have wondered about the five-pointed star, even at that time the symbol of young Soviet Russia. The three spires and stars may have suggested the ancient doctrine of the Trinity, native to the Far East, which theosophists and anthroposophists aimed at renewing. But above all Gropius' words against "class-dividing arrogance", for "a new coming faith", and a "building of the future" embracing all the arts, gave hope to all those young people who had been robbed of their illusions. Gropius' idea of a return to the crafts could also be interpreted as a romantic encouragement to the individual craftsman in deliberate opposition to the "art industry" which had flourished before the war.

The training programme of the new *Bauhaus* in Weimar differed from the proclamation. It was more objective and far from romantic. Those able to read it properly realised that with the "building of the future" Gropius did not refer to an actual building, and that *Bauhaus* did not mean a school for builders. It rather meant building the future of artistically talented people for the benefit of the whole community. "The aim was to be the training of skilled craftsmen or independent artists, on the basis of a craftsman's apprenticeship." This apprenticeship would not take the form of arts-and-crafts work, but was to be the regular training of a joiner, blacksmith, stone-mason, potter, weaver, bookbinder or painter, with an examination for "journeyman standard" before the State Chamber of Handicrafts. It was Gropius' intention to combine this practical workshop training with a training conditioning the student to an understanding of material, colour and form. This part of the training was to be the work of the *Formmeister*. The appointment of these artists, together with the idea of a dual training, were to be the germ of the actual *Bauhaus* doctrine which, later on, was to have such far-reaching results.

It is true that with the curriculum Gropius continued in the art college tradition, but he also gave to apprenticeship a much wider meaning. He took into account the whole human being, on the one hand as a craftsman who knew his work down to the basic materials and tools, and on the other as a creative artist. German arts-and-crafts schools since the beginning of the twentieth century had recognised the importance of technical training. They had also kept their own training workshops, though design on paper and aesthetic theory still took up much of the time.

The beginnings of this movement lay in Britain where the disastrous effects of the exploitation of the machine first showed. Also there, the problems of "applied art and the machine", or "applied art by the machine", or "applied art for the machine" were first considered. From these considerations arose experiments to define art from the sociological point of view, instead of the old approach via philosophy and aesthetics. William Morris was the most important representative in the movement for improving standards, all supported by a hazy socialism. Morris saw the disaster which nineteenth-century capitalism and "the ways of Manchester" were causing by their ruthless use of machines, precipitating the fall of the craftsman, the loss of pleasure in work through exploitation, and the mass production of rubbish. In an effort to stop the rot Morris founded an association which, under the guidance of creative artists, supplied paintings, wood-carvings, furniture and metal utensils made by craftsmen. Morris hoped that the creative artist, through joining with others, and producing articles of quality, would be taken out of his isolation as a pure academic, and find his function in everyday life. However, Morris' opposition to the machine, his deliberate limitation to hand-made articles, made his output uneconomical. Though an avowed enemy of capitalism, Morris had to find buyers for his association's output among the rich, as his hand-made articles were very expensive. The products of his hand-printing press, the Kelmscott Press, were perfect examples of type-setting, printing, paper, illustrations and binding, but only those who could afford forty to a hundred shillings for a book could enjoy the results. That sum was the weekly wage of a good workman or the salary of a higher employee. Quite contrary to Morris' idea about art only being important if all could share in it, his opposition to using machines, and to mass production, led him to being exclusive. All the same, it will remain his lasting merit to have stimulated artistic design in objects of daily use. Good textile prints, handsome wallpapers, good type for printing, fine bookbinding spread out from his association, and even penetrated – against Morris' original intention – to mass production.

Charles Robert Ashbee went one step further in the direction towards the basic principles of the future *Bauhaus*. Like Morris a British socialist, he took up Morris' ideas, but did not share his hatred of the machine. He wanted to "put the machine in its place", limiting its usefulness to mass production. All creative production was to return to the workshop of the individual craftsman. The work of the craftsman or artist-craftsman should stand side by side with the output of the machine, but not compete with it. Ashbee's Guild for Wood- and Metal-Work, founded in London in 1901, was to be an association of individual craftsmen, producing quality goods. Its training workshops had the task of resisting the deteriorating standards of contemporary training. This was the first work-shop to possess the character of a school. Before that the practical training of the craftsman took place in a master's workshop. This training, like the master's workshop itself, suffered from the pressures of machine pro-duction. With Ashbee's Guild the trade union idea of modern times took the place of Morris' romantic-medieval notion of the union of craftsmen.

The stimulating effect of Ashbee's initiative is not minimized by the fact that after seven years his Guild went bankrupt, with a deficit of six thousand pounds. Ashbee's theories were taken up in Germany. As early as 1895 the Grand Duke of Hesse had asked Ashbee to execute designs for work at his castle in Darmstadt. Ashbee's ideas of associations of artists and artists' colonies made a lasting impression there.

More important, however, than this contact of Ashbee's and other British and Belgian reformers with German princely patrons, was the direct influence of British work on architects in Central Europe. At the beginning of the twentieth century the German architect, Hermann Muthesius, made the "English house" and its interior the subject of his special study. During his years in Britain he became well acquainted with Ashbee's aspirations. He recognised the significance of the guild idea and also the reasons for its economic failure. In Prussia he tried therefore to reform existing institutions rather than risk entirely new foundations. The high official position Muthesius held in Prussia at the beginning of the twentieth century enabled him to influence art schools in the appointment of young and able architects as directors (Peter Behrens in Düsseldorf, Hans Poelzig in Breslau, Bruno Paul in Berlin). On Ashbee's pattern he started training workshops where students of the arts-and-crafts schools could familiarise themselves with tools and materials, instead of designing only on paper, and employing themselves mainly with the study and history of styles, and aesthetics. Hermann Muthesius also tried to come to terms with the problem of "art and the machine". As an architect he copied the functionalism of building engineering though this still tended to hide essentials behind ornaments and false façades. It was only the new theories the gifted Viennese architect, Adolf Loos, worked out in his publication *Ornament und Verbrechen*, 1906, which opened the eyes of technical engineers to the falsity of their disguising a steel or steel-and-concrete skeleton by Renaissance or *Jugendstil* ornament.

For Germany the year 1907 marked the beginning of a new relationship between manufacturers and their machines, craftsmen and their quality work, and artists and their conception of form. The cabinet-maker, Karl Schmidt, commissioned the Berlin architect, Bruno Paul, to design furniture for the *Deutsche Werkstätten* in Dresden. This furniture was then offered at an astonishingly low price as mass production, and as an example of "a style of furniture grown from the spirit of the machine age". Even more important was a connection formed, also in 1907, by one of the largest industrial concerns of the period, Emil Rathenau's *Allgemeine Elektrizitäts-Gesellschaft* (A.E.G.) in Berlin. Their director, Jordan, commissioned the architect Peter Behrens to do work for A.E.G. Behrens then designed the famous turbine factory, the assembly shops and the workers' settlements in Berlin, as well as the models for mass-produced street lamps, table lamps, ceiling light fittings and publicity material, letter heads, share certificates and diplomas. Eventually he also designed the fittings for A.E.G.'s Berlin retail shops.

These isolated cases of private initiative in trying to tackle the problems of mass production and work of the craftsman or individual artist, in time found effective expression in the *Deutscher Werkbund*, founded in 1907 on the instigation of Hermann Muthesius. As laid down in its statutes, the *Bund* was to unite "artists, craftsmen, experts and patrons, intent on an improvement of production through collaboration of art, industry and the crafts, through training, publicity and the forming of a united front".

Membership of the *Werkbund* was by invitation only, following a resolution by the council, and members could be expelled for an offence against the interests of the association. Soon the *Werkbund* became an important factor in the cultural life of Germany. It reached its peak in the Cologne *Werkbund* exhibition of 1914, suspended, however, on the outbreak of war. In spite of the *Werkbund's* importance from 1907 to 1914, nothing like a *Werkbund* style evolved. In the *Bund* as elsewhere – generally speaking – the three main artistic tendencies of the day were of equal interest: there was the functional view, aiming at a clear design, with some designers' work reminiscent of a classical style, there was *Jugendstil*, though this had fallen into disrepute by the time the *Werkbund* was founded, through misuse by designers, craftsmen and manufacturers, and finally there was a reactionary trend, imitating a style of the "good old days", in this case the years of the *Biedermeier*, between 1820 and 1840.

Gropius belonged to the young representatives of the functional group of the *Werkbund*, not dependent on classical influences. Born in Berlin, into a family of stage technicians and architects, he was well disposed towards technical developments in building, and he rejected *Jugendstil* and *Neo-Biedermeier*. From 1907 to 1910 he worked as an assistant in Peter Behrens' Berlin office, during the designing period for A.E.G. Here Gropius was strongly led towards industrial architecture and designing for industrial mass production. In Behrens' office he met and learnt to respect Adolf Meyer who later on for fifteen years was his collaborator and assistant. He began in Gropius' own office when it was opened in Berlin in 1910.

With his first work, the Fagus Shoe-Tree Factory in Alfeld/Leine, designed with Meyer in 1911, Gropius created the prototype of an honest building. Since a steel frame made a supporting wall unnecessary, Gropius drew the logical conclusion, and replaced the wall by sheets of glass. With this work Gropius soon moved into the top rank of artists trying to educate the public by means of the *Werkbund*. These intentions were probably encouraged by the two years older Meyer who by origin and career differed completely from him. Meyer came from the Eifel, was trained as a joiner, and had been a student at the Düsseldorf School of Arts and Crafts under Behrens' directorship. There he had become interested in architecture, and had been specially attached to the Dutch architect Lauweriks who taught at Düsseldorf. Through him Meyer was introduced to theosophy. One might say that to Gropius Meyer presented the ideal of what later became the *Bauhaus* type of man: he had turned to architecture and building techniques after a craftsman's training, and in addition to this, his strong personality had been shaped by a religious-philosophical doctrine.

In the yearbooks of the *Deutscher Werkbund* for 1913 and 1914, prepared in the preceding years, Gropius took up his position clearly and precisely. In an article of 1913, on "The development of modern industrial architecture", Gropius said: "An object of even technical perfection must be imbued with spiritual content and with form, so that it becomes outstanding in the multitude of similar objects." The following year, on the subject of "The style-forming value of industrial architecture", he pointed for the first time to sociological and ethical factors in creative art. His article begins: "The art of past decades lacked a moral focus, and therefore the condition essential for fruitful development", and he ended by saying that the more the spirit of the age expanded, overcoming all obstacles, the more would all our activities be reflected in a common image. Only when the great blessings of a new faith was given again to mankind, he thought, would art once more fulfill its true function, the ornamenting of works of pure functionalism with gay creation.

When six years later Gropius again raised his voice in the world of German art, his optimism, his hope for European unity of expression had been destroyed by the battles of the First World War. The idea of influencing industry and crafts through the *Deutscher Werkbund*, so effective between 1907 and 1914, seemed remote. So was the possibility of forming a working community of industry, craftsmen and creative artists. During the war years industry and crafts – almost without exception – had been drawn into armament production, and questions of design were given no consideration.

In November 1918, the month of the German revolution, artists in Berlin founded the *Novembergruppe*, a "Works Council for Art". Here Gropius met creative artists who had left the ranks of "academic art" years ago. They were the painters Lyonel Feininger, Otto Mueller, Erich Heckel, Karl Schmidt-Rottluff, Christian Rohlfs, the sculptors Rudolf Belling, Gerhard Marcks, and the architects Otto Bartning, Erich Mendelsohn, Hans Poelzig and Bruno Taut. This circle, with its manifesto *Ja. Stimmen des Arbeitsrates für Kunst in Berlin*, took, early in 1919, the line which rebel artists had repeatedly taken since Marinetti's futurist manifesto of February 1909. They addressed the public in a passionate proclamation, its revolutionary layout matching the contents. The manifesto *Ja* showed a woodcut by Lyonel Feininger on its title page. The prospectus for the exhibition of the "Works Council for Art", *Unbekannte Architekten*, of April 1919, was also in the character of a manifesto. In this folder which, too, was decorated by a symbolic design, Gropius spoke again publicly about architects and architecture of the future. "There are no architects today, we are all preparing the way for the one who some day will merit this name again. That name implies 'Master of the Art', one who will make gardens out of deserts, and let miracles rise to the sky."

The third manifesto, of 1919, was the most important. It was Gropius' proclamation and programme of the Weimar *Bauhaus*, issued in April 1919, aimed at the provisional government of Thuringia. Gropius declared that the *Bauhaus* presented a combination of the Academy of Fine Art and the former School of Arts and Crafts, with a new Department of Architecture. This was, of course, only partly true. In actual fact, the combination meant only the taking over of budgets and buildings of the two schools, as well as the teaching staff of the Academy, including the painters Otto Fröhlich, Walther Klemm and Max Thedy, and the sculptor Richard Engelmann. Nothing was left of the School of Arts and Crafts, officially closed in 1915, but the weaving and bookbinding workshops which had become privately owned and were working in rented schoolrooms. The staff had been dismissed in 1915, and workshop fittings were sold off cheaply. Of these two schools which, according to Gropius' proclamation, were the basis of his new foundation, the Academy had a good reputation, with its teaching staff of Theodor Hagen, Hans Olde, Ludwig von Hofmann, Walther Klemm, and Richard Engelmann. Max Beckmann, Jean Arp, Hans Richter, Carlo Mense, Ivo Hauptmann, Theo Champion, Gert Wollheim, Otto Pankok, Otto Herbig and Ernst Penzoldt had all been its students at one time or another. The School of Arts and Crafts had developed from a private school Henry van de Velde had built up from 1902, after his appointment as artistic adviser to arts and industries in the Grand Duchy of Saxe-Weimar-Eisenach. Up to the beginning of the First World War the school had been an important factor in the economic life of the region. Van de Velde had managed to aggrandise his private school into a state-owned building in Weimar, designed by him. Then, after 1 March 1908 it became the Grand Ducal School of Arts and Crafts. No distinct division existed at the school between private work and privately owned workshops on the one hand, and school activities and school workshops on the other. There had been training workshops for bookbinding and metal work. A printing workshop was van de Velde's private property. The weaving workshop belonged to the *Paulinenstiftung für gewerblichen Hausfleiss* – a foundation, the carpet-weaving studio to the teacher, Li Thorn, and the goldsmith and enamel workshop to the teachers, Wibiral and Seligmüller. Van de Velde's work and that of his teachers and students was based on crafts. This work was no longer done in opposition to industry and mass production. It rather followed Ashbee's ideas of individual craftsmanship, competing economically with mass production, but rising above it by its special quality. With extensive private offices, fully staffed, which van de Velde kept at the school, and with the prevailing private character of the training workshops the profit motive was of prime importance at the School of Arts and Crafts. The collaboration of the school workshops with big commercial firms in Weimar and surroundings proved very profitable to jewellers, blacksmiths, woodworkers, workers in leathercraft, bookbinders and teachers alike. Van de Velde had been appointed to Weimar at a salary of four thousand marks, but he himself stated that his income there, during the years just preceding the First World War, had been eighty to one hundred thousand marks, on top of his salary. When towards 1908 Grand Duke Wilhelm Ernst of Weimar lost interest in cultural work, and even took a dislike to van de Velde and his circle, the position of this artist became difficult. Nationalistic tendencies were exploited against van de Velde, the foreigner. It became a question of "regional art" against "internationalism", "native art" against "French decadence". It all led to van de Velde tending his resignation in July 1914, for October of that year. The outbreak of war cut short plans for continuing the school under a new director. Instead, it was closed officially on 1 October 1915. The staff was dismissed, the school workshops closed and their equipment dispersed. However, the painter, Fritz Mackensen, director of the Academy of Fine Art, promoted a plan for making the School of Arts and Crafts a department of his Academy, with the addition of a Department of Architecture. The whole school was to be under his direction. Van de Velde himself named Walter Gropius and Hermann Obrist as suitable successors. Thereupon Gropius had an audience with the Grand Duke in Weimar, and following it, he suggested combining the two art schools under his direction. In a memorandum of January 1916 he sketched a plan, according to his own principles, for work in the new school. This institution was not to train independent artists, as had done the Academy of Fine Art, nor was it to produce arts-and-crafts goods as did the workshops of the School of Arts and Crafts. Gropius wished to train the artist "to come to terms with the most powerful means of modern production, the machine, from the simple tool to the most specialised machinery". He wanted the artist to learn to make the machine his servant. To achieve a collaboration between artist and industry Gropius visualised a body of students consisting of young skilled craftsmen or draughtsmen, sent by their firms to attend. In that way they would keep in touch with their factory or their master's workshop, and continue to do practical work there. To this the school would add the study of materials, form and composition. The memorandum of 1916 did not envisage school workshops nor the production – in the school – of arts-and-crafts goods, paintings, sculptures or architectural work. The aim was rather, in the words of Gropius, "the stimulation of all the arts and crafts", and the forming of "a happy working community such as had existed in an ideal way in the masons' lodges of the Middle Ages".*

* Hans Maria Wingler, *Das Bauhaus*. Bramsche 1963, p. 29

This memorandum, at least its main contents, became known to the teaching staff of the Academy of Fine Art, and was taken by them as being directed against their own work. Mackensen had previously thought of Gropius as the head of a Department of Architecture, of his combined schools, but now a new proposal from the staff of professors, of 12 December 1917, suggested filling the vacant positions of the suspended School of Arts and Crafts – under the directorship of Mackensen – by Willy Jäckel for decorative painting, Thorn-Prikker for stained glass, Karl Walser for stage craft, Zutt for medals and small arts and crafts, and Max Berg for architecture. The staff, making these proposals, consisted of Theodor Hagen, Max Thedy, Walther Klemm and Richard Engelmann, under the chairmanship of Fritz Mackensen. However, no definite decisions were taken because of the war. The post of the director of the Academy of Fine Art became vacant too when, in the summer of 1918, Mackensen handed in his resignation for 1 October. When Ducal rule ended in November 1918, and a provisional government of the new "land" Thuringia took over, the School of Arts and Crafts was still in suspension, with five teaching vacancies, and no director had been appointed to the Academy of Fine Art.

It is necessary to explain this situation fully for an understanding of the tactics used by Gropius in the founding of the *Bauhaus*. The question of administration was a very complicated one. To begin with, it was not clear who was entitled to appoint new directors and teachers for the two art schools. Side by side with the provisional government, and in spite of the Grand Duke's formal abdication, his Lord Chamberlain's office, under Freiherr von Fritsch, was still effective, in so far as it administered the making of appointments and the allotting of money from the Grand Ducal educational and arts funds.

On the advice of the director of the theatre, Ernst Hardt, and the director of the museum, Dr. Wilhelm Koehler, in Weimar, Gropius then turned, in January 1919, to Freiherr von Fritsch, with regard to his being appointed director of the joint art schools. Von Fritsch asked Wilhelm von Bode, director of the Berlin museums, for advice, and received a reply much in Gropius' favour. The teaching staff of the Academy of Fine Art, alert to the new situation, asked the Lord Chamberlain's office, in February 1919, to appoint Gropius as director. At the same time Weimar's industry and trades asked the education department of the provisional government to appoint van de Velde as director of the Academy of Fine Art, and to create at that school a chair for arts and crafts and architecture, to be occupied by Walter Gropius. Earlier on he had agreed to accept such an appointment. The Lord Chamberlain's office, encouraged by Wilhelm von Bode's approval, and aware of the dislike of the former Grand Duke for van de Velde, stuck to Gropius. After a discussion between von Fritsch and the State Commissioner,

Baudert, on 16 March 1919, the Lord Chamberlain's office used the right it still possessed, and appointed Gropius director of the Academy of Fine Art. Certain of his appointment, Gropius asked, on 20 March 1919, the deputy director, Max Thedy, to make an application to the provisional government, on behalf of the teaching staff, for the renaming of the combined schools. The new name was to be *Staatliches Bauhaus in Weimar* (uniting the former Grand Ducal Academy of Fine Art with the Grand Ducal School of Arts and Crafts).

It is uncertain on which day and by whom Gropius was officially appointed director of the *Staatliches Bauhaus*. Through his Weimar advisers he probably had good knowledge of the confused situation regarding competence and the actual and alleged rights of the provisional government, the State Commissioner and the Lord Chamberlain's office, and made use of this vague situation to bring the suspended School of Arts and Crafts back into existence, combining it with the Academy of Fine Art, and, at the same time, gain control over existing vacancies and potentialities of the two institutions. Prudently and diplomatically Gropius negotiated, now as director of the *Bauhaus*, with the two authorities, the socialist provisional government and the Lord Chamberlain's office. On 15 April 1919 he submitted a new statute; on 22 May he named officially Max Thedy, Walther Klemm, Richard Engelmann and Otto Fröhlich as old teachers, and Lyonel Feininger, Johannes Itten and Gerhard Marcks as new ones. He stated that two further chairs had not been filled meanwhile. With an application to the Lord Chamberlain's office, of 2 May, Gropius tried to increase the space of the new school. He asked for the use of the former riding school on the Ilm, which for decades had served the Ducal Court as a place for storing tools, superfluous furniture and paintings from the castles. No reply was received up to April 1921, then came a refusal. A new application of December 1919 to the Lord Chamberlain, von Fritsch, for an audience with the Grand Duke, with the object of asking personally for the *Römisches Haus* in the park, as a studio for a *Bauhaus* teacher, was refused at once.

By appointing Lyonel Feininger, Gropius had lost the sympathy of circles close to the Lord Chamberlain's office, and of the Weimar reactionaries. The new teachers, Johannes Itten and Gerhard Marcks, escaped notice since they were unknown quantities. To begin with, Gropius' opponents were careful. It was generally believed that the Grand Duke, while still in power, had initiated or at least intended Gropius' appointment, and that von Fritsch had made the actual appointment not only with the agreement of the State Commissioner, Baudert, but above all in agreement with the former Grand Duke.

When Fritz Mackensen, former director of the Academy of Fine Art, declared publicly that it had never been the

Grand Duke's intention to appoint Gropius as his, Mackensen's, successor, the opposition became more determined. Freiherr von Fritsch, who had meantime retired from his official post, hastened to declare that he had appointed Gropius only on von Bode's recommendation in agreement with the State Commissioner, without either consulting or informing the Grand Duke, and that neither the name of *Bauhaus* nor the combining of the two schools and the new statutes had been sanctioned.

This combining of the two schools not only supported Gropius' idea of the supremacy of architecture, it was also sound organisation. The suspended School of Arts and Crafts had at its disposal funds from various sources, which had not been used since the closing of the school. At a time when devaluation of the German currency was not yet thought of, and the rising cost of living was considered a passing phase, these funds seemed quite substantial. Also, the vacancies at the suspended school gave Gropius an opportunity for making new appointments. This made it unnecessary to try out new ideas with a teaching staff taken over from the Academy of Fine Art. Without commenting on their abilities, it must be said that each as a painter, graphic artist or sculptor was too academic to become a *Formmeister* – in Gropius' sense. This could still have applied if Georg Kolbe had been proposed in place of Richard Engelmann, Lovis Corinth in place of Thedy, and perhaps even Max Slevogt for Walther Klemm. It was not a question of age either, for Gropius was of the same age as Klemm. Engelmann was fifty-four years old, still two years younger than Kandinsky when he started his work at the *Bauhaus*. What Gropius was looking for, and what he found in the new teachers he appointed, were men with an untraditional perception of the world, openmindedness, artistic universality, and joy in experimenting. Also, he wanted his staff to be free from traditional ideas of labelling according to rank – fine art at the top, then the lesser "applied" arts and crafts, with mass production at the bottom.

Gropius first appointed Lyonel Feininger, Gerhard Marcks and Johannes Itten. Feininger had for years worked in "applied" art, as caricaturist with the Berlin *Ulk*. He carved and put together intricate models of yachts, grotesque railways, miniature houses and towns. He also was an able pianist and composer of fugues. Feininger was no stranger to Weimar. From 1906–1914 he had a studio in 7 a Kurthstrasse in Weimar. He had worked there in the spring or summer of 1906, 1911, 1913 and 1914, and had cycled a lot to the small villages of the neighbourhood, making drawings of the life they lived. His closer acquaintance with Gropius, and the start of their friendship dated back to their joint work in the Berlin *Novembergruppe* during the winter of 1918/19.

Gropius had known Gerhard Marcks, the teacher appointed second, longer. Marcks worked as a sculptor, but not as an exclusively independent artist. He made models for porcelain figures, and had worked happily in the service of architecture, when in 1914 he created the ceramic wall decorations for the restaurant, built by Gropius and Meyer for the exhibition of the *Deutscher Werkbund* in Cologne. He had also met Gropius again, after the war, in the winter of 1918/19, among the members of the *Novembergruppe*. In the *Bauhaus* Marcks' work of making models was an important contribution to the teachings of the school.

Johannes Itten was the only one of the *Bauhaus* teachers with previous educational experience. He was exceptional both as an artist and teacher. As a Swiss elementary school teacher he had been exposed early to the theory of "Learning by Doing". His mathematical and scientific studies, combined with the study of the theory of art, form and colour under Adolf Hölzel in Stuttgart, later became the basis for his own theory of art education. From 1916 till his appointment in Weimar, he was director of a private art school in Vienna. During this time he exhibited his own work in the *Sturm* at Berlin. His contacts with Gropius were, however, not made in Berlin, but in Vienna where lived Gropius' first wife, Frau Alma, widow of the composer, Gustav Mahler. There, in the circle around Franz Werfel, Oskar Kokoschka, Adolf Loos, and the musicians and Mahler disciples, Arnold Schönberg and Alban Berg, the association with Itten began, and eventually led to his appointment. Itten was a strong masterful personality, and a number of his Viennese students followed their "master" to Weimar.

Compared to Itten, Feininger and Marcks, even Gropius himself, were apparently at a disadvantage because of their lack of educational training. But on the other hand, their unconventional performances became the very essence of that creative activity, which was to be an important ingredient of the *Bauhaus* spirit and, from 1923 onwards, exerted a steadily growing influence on general design. Gropius had made no mistake in appointing outstanding artists, even if they never gave a thought to instruction in the way the old academies had done by "correcting" students' work.

During the first years, however, it often looked as if the *Bauhaus* might be wrecked through differences among its *Formmeister*, all the more so as things were not very satisfactory with regard to the technical masters and the training in the workshops. Even the most elementary matters had to be thought of during the hunger years of the post-war period. They influenced the life of the *Bauhaus*. During its first summer Gropius encouraged friends and patrons to make donations to a *Bauhaus* fund. From April to October 1919 he could gratefully acknowledge nearly one million marks, compared to an annual salary of the ten masters of altogether sixty-seven thousand marks. Barely two years later, through the devaluation of the mark, the fund diminished to practically nothing, but till then it was most useful. The *Bauhaus* kitchen offered a large number of *Bauhaus* students the only possibility of affording a midday and evening meal. It was natural for Gropius and other teachers to eat there too. This "workshop habit", as Gropius liked to call it, may have been common also in other places. But it was only possible at Gropius' *Bauhaus* that masters such as Feininger, Klee, Itten, Marcks, Muche, Schlemmer and Schreyer gave works of art, to be auctioned at the Berlin *Sturm* in December 1921, in aid of a *Bauhaus* fund.

To see everything in proportion it is necessary to look carefully at the general situation in Germany and Weimar in the years from 1919–1921. This will prevent misjudgement of an important personality like Itten, whose influence on students and teachers Gropius was eventually forced to curb, when he was leading them into opposition to Gropius' own ideas. This important incident in the history of the Weimar *Bauhaus* only becomes understandable if the intellectual atmosphere in Germany after the First World War is remembered. The starving and freezing young people from the schoolrooms or training workshops had only known "life" in battles and trenches. After the end of the war they were offered doctrines of salvation by many prophets and leaders. Itten was a disciple of such a doctrine, of the teachings of Mazdaism. Based on the Persian teachings of Zoroaster, it aimed at reform and a new humanity. This in itself would not have been alien to *Bauhaus* ideas where Gropius himself worked in perfect harmony with Meyer who was a follower of theosophy. But Itten and his circle among the students were obsessed by their doctrine. In the obligatory preliminary course under Itten's leadership, minerals, plants and animals were studied. Colours were investigated and so were geometrical forms, and these were pointed out as elements of all masterpieces of past ages. In these studies it was stressed that contemplation and meditation must play a part over and above perception by the senses and the brain. Acceptance or refusal of such ideas became an argument which might decide admission to Itten's preliminary course, and so to the Bauhaus itself. Though Gropius had stated in the *Bauhaus* manifesto that the *Meisterrat* – the Council of the Masters – would decide about admission, soon a Students' Council, made up of Itten's fanatical followers, was formed, trying to make its own decisions. Certainly this council did not function over all admissions, also its decisions were not necessarily binding, but that such a "sifting" was possible at a state school in Central Europe in 1919/20 is remarkable in itself. One of the *Bauhaus* students, Helmut von Erffa, wrote: "It was not easy to get oneself accepted for his (Itten's) preliminary course which prepared one for the workshops. After we had had an interview with Gropius, we still had to be passed by a kind of one-man Student Council. I remember my trepidation as I was led into the room, whitewashed and totally bare, except for a huge black wooden cross on one wall. On a simple iron bedstead sat a haggard young man in a monk's habit. His cheeks were hollow, his eyes burnt feverishly. He was one of Itten's most trusted pupils. 'Really a saint,' my companion whispered. The young man looked me over while my companion stood in respectful silence, then he said something in an ecstatic sing-song voice and nodded. He had seen none of my drawings and barely heard me utter a word but I had passed the test and was accepted. 'The master has complete trust in his intuitive judgement,' my companion explained after we had left the room."*

Itten's preliminary course included dietetics, breathing exercises, training in meditation, and, as can be seen by the "examination", was based on a *Weltanschauung* seeking to penetrate to extra-sensory perception. Consciously or subconsciously Itten and his followers worked towards submitting the whole of the *Bauhaus* to their doctrine. For some time the *Bauhaus* kitchen actually cooked food only according to the teachings of Mazdaism. Itten further strengthened his influence by bringing to Weimar Gertrud Grunow, and making it possible for her to introduce to the *Bauhaus* her Studies in Harmony. Gertrud Grunow, then fifty years old, seems to have been a woman of strong spiritual force, who in some cases exercised a beneficial influence on the disturbed state of mind of young people. Other students found her exercises most odd. In a trance-like state colours, sounds and shapes were meditated on. In the early days of the *Bauhaus* the only regular training in meditation was done in Itten's preliminary course and in Gertrud Grunow's Studies in Harmony. It is interesting to read what Werner Gräff, a *Bauhaus* "renegade", has to say: "Itten, an educationist, full of ideas, also had his weaknesses. He was, of course, free to belong to a sect himself – Mazdaism, an American doctrine of salvation taking up ancient Persian ideas – but it is doubtful whether factual teaching should have been mixed up with life-reforming or religious ideas in such a way. When songs, utterly trashy to me, were to be sung for breathing exercises, I could stand it no longer."**

The preliminary course, as such, had however not run into special difficulties because of Itten's unusual teaching experience. It was rather the much stressed workshop training which met with almost insurmountable obstacles during the first and second year. The first exhibition of students' work in June 1919, consisted only of paintings, mainly by students and members of the former Academy of Fine Art. On this occasion Gropius remarked:

* Helmut von Erffa, *Bauhaus. First Phase.* London 1957

** Werner Gräff, *Katalog der Ausstellung des Kunstvereins Rheinland-Westfalen.* Düsseldorf 1962

"I propose not to have a public exhibition for some time, and meantime to make a fresh start in our work."*
With this he promised, for the autumn of 1919, a transformation of the *Bauhaus*, and a clearing up of the question
who was entitled to call himself "apprentice", "journeyman" or "young master", terms which had been banded
about, without being backed by a sound training in craftsmanship.

To create this necessary basis it seemed natural to consider the workshops, left intact, by van de Velde's Weimar
School of Arts and Crafts: the weaving workshop and the bookbindery, now owned by former teachers. Therefore Gropius tried to find *Formmeister* for these workshops. On the advice of a Weimar painter, Johannes Molzahn, he appointed the young Berlin artist, Georg Muche, to the *Bauhaus* – not as *Formmeister* for economic
reasons, but as assistant to Itten in the preliminary course. Unofficially, however, Muche took on work as
*Formmeister* in the weaving workshop. This workshop then got well organised, thanks to the accommodating
nature of Helene Börner, who had already taught under van de Velde, with Muche as *Formmeister* and Helene
Börner as technical master, according to Gropius' plan. The early stages were difficult only because Muche was
opposed to Gropius' idea of the interdependence of the crafts and fine art. He therefore did not concern himself
with the technical side of weaving, and limited his own teaching to free creative work with brush and etching-
needle. It was, however, to the advantage of the workshop that some experienced women artists like Ida Kerko-
vius and Margarete Bittkow turned to weaving. They were able to transfer Muche's ideas to the medium of
textile work. Soon, too, the weaving workshop saw the special talents of the young Gunta Stölzl develop.

Gerhard Marcks was *Formmeister* in the pottery. Through his models of animals for the Schwarzburg porcelain
manufactory, and his ceramic work for Gropius' building at the *Werkbund* exhibition of 1914 in Cologne, he had
a feeling for the craft. However, an experiment in using the kilns of the Weimar makers of stoves, Schmidt, for
*Bauhaus* training, failed. With the work of *Bauhaus* apprentices, begun in the autumn of 1919, at the factory, it
soon became obvious that these privately owned works were not suitable as training ground, even less for experimenting. Gropius and Marcks therefore abandoned this work in the spring of 1920, and tried instead to rent
a small workshop. The re-establishment of a pottery workshop was impossible for lack of funds and space.
However, no suitable workshop became available in Weimar, nor in the nearby little potters' town of Bürgel
whose small independent master-potters were impervious to the *Bauhaus* idea of a dual apprenticeship under a

* Walther Scheidig, *Die Weimarer Malerschule. Ausstellungskatalog.* Weimar 1960, pp. 57–61

*Formmeister* and a technical master. At last a workshop was found in Dornburg on the Saale, twenty-five kilometres from Weimar and ten kilometres from Jena. It was owned by a master-potter, Max Krehan, last member of an old family of potters. In Dornburg the stables of the little Rococo castle, now state-owned, supplied the necessary space for the training workshop with technical installations and kilns. Marcks and his apprentices moved to Dornburg.

The background of this workshop was good as Krehan worked in the traditional, almost folk-art manner, supplying the needs of the little rural town and countryside around, unaffected by designers or reformers of the late nineteenth or early twentieth century. His workshop was an ideal place for getting familiar with ordinary raw materials, the potter's wheel, and a simple kiln. In addition, the school workshop at the castle made it possible to apply knowledge, gained at the wheel, by experimenting in the creative atmosphere of Marcks' teaching. Here students could expand.

Similar to the weaving workshop, the pottery too had the advantage of having as one of Marcks' apprentices a sculptor of some experience. Otto Lindig was only six years younger than Marcks. He had been trained with the Thuringian porcelain manufacturers of Lichte and Ilmenau, and had come to Weimar in 1913, to study at van de Velde's School of Arts and Crafts. When this school was closed, he transferred, in November 1915, to Engelmann's sculpture class at the Academy of Fine Art. There he received in 1917 his diploma and a studio of his own. All the same, he accompanied Marcks as an "apprentice" to Dornburg. At the age of twenty-seven he took his examination as a "journeyman"-potter before the Chamber of Handicrafts. The distance between Weimar and Dornburg brought about some isolation for Marcks and his pottery workshop. Looking back, it appears that this was useful to the *Bauhaus*. Removed from the ideological differences and fashions which kept sweeping the school, a more down-to-earth atmosphere could prevail. It is not mere chance that the first *Bauhaus* designs for industry came from this pottery.

At the school workshop *Formmeister* and apprentices, including Lindig and soon also the talented Theo Bogler, were not contented working with potter's clay, lead glazing and low firing. They transferred to an earthen-ware type of material which, at a high temperature, produced a hard close texture with no need for glazing. This material then made it possible to leave the design entirely to the artist. It allowed for rims as sharp as metal, and with the new process, Otto Lindig developed his "convex" rims. These, together with the special *Bauhaus* handle, were often imitated.

Lyonel Feininger, the third of Gropius' early appointed teachers, was not *Formmeister* to a special workshop. In the summer of 1920 Gropius invited Oskar Schlemmer to collaborate, without being attached, in the meantime, to a workshop. Schlemmer had come to Weimar at that time to negotiate about the publication of his graphic work in the annual *Utopia*. This publication was being prepared by Johannes Itten and Dr. Bruno Adler. Schlemmer's first impressions of Gropius and the *Bauhaus* were: "They want to do much, but can do nothing for lack of funds. So they play about ... It is incredible, for example, that the excellent workshop fittings were sold during the war, so that now there is scarcely a planing-bench, and that in an institution based on the crafts."* Nevertheless, attracted by the idea of the *Bauhaus*, Schlemmer accepted a teaching appointment in December 1920. Paul Klee came to Weimar at the same time. The previous year Schlemmer with the whole Students' Council had tried in vain to have Klee appointed to the Stuttgart Academy.

The wood-working shop, of which Schlemmer had said that it hardly possessed a bench, was under the personal direction of Gropius, to begin with, with Joseph Zackmann as technical master. In his workshop as elsewhere Gropius counted on longish periods of preparation. Though Gropius as an architect tended to architectural cubist designs in furniture, he was willing to accept fantastic, even symbolic, shapes as long as they demanded a high degree of technical skill. At that time Gropius did not consider offering to industry the experiments of his workshop. It appears that in the beginning wood-carving was closely linked to the wood-working shop. There was no separate technical master or *Formmeister* in the wood-carving workshop. It made do with an artist turned "apprentice", the painter Joost Schmidt, who, from 1910–1914, had been a student of the Weimar Academy, to become a *Bauhaus* apprentice in 1919. Wood-carving, in particular, had to deal with much work in the first year of the *Bauhaus*. This was not work according to the school curriculum, but a welcome chance to give needy students an opportunity for earning money. As a private commission Gropius was building a wooden house for Adolf Sommerfeld, a timber specialist, in Berlin-Dahlem. With work on the exterior and interior of this timber house Gropius gave *Bauhaus* apprentices and journeymen a good chance for paid collaboration. According to the nature of the building, wood-carving played a major part in the interior. The "apprentice", Joost Schmidt, undertook this work from his own designs. He made in the *Bauhaus* workshops carved doors, decorations on staircases, and casings for heating. A few pieces of furniture, especially easy chairs with covers of red and black morocco,

* Oskar Schlemmer, *Briefe und Tagebücher*. Munich 1958, p. 94. 13. 7. 1920

were apprentice work of Marcel Breuer. They were of cubist design, and appeared a little odd in an interior dominated by the linear character of expressionism. The lamps, door-handles and other fittings were also made by *Bauhaus* students, for the most part entirely by hand. Nowhere is there a trace of industrial design. But since Gropius himself was at that time working towards furniture design of simple straight lines, and his students, Marcel Breuer, Erich Dickmann and Joseph Albers, followed his example in their first outstanding work during their apprenticeship, *Haus Sommerfeld*, with its interior and furnishings, cannot be taken as a typical *Bauhaus* product. It does, however, show that Gropius, for the sake of artistic liberty, allowed his teachers and students to express themselves freely. This might be through designs derived from futurism, the *Sturm* or dadaism. He was right in believing that time would work in his favour, and show the importance of a training of the whole personality as a basis for a future community of creative workers. Apprentices of the first years, such as Albers, Breuer, Bogler, Lindig, Scheper, Joost Schmidt and Stölzl, completely justified Gropius' hope of being able to have no division between *Formmeister* and technical masters in a few years' time. He hoped by then to have available people with both faculties developed equally. However, he was not given a chance to let his ideas mature. Gropius had to spend his days fighting for money from the State, for working space for the school, places to live in for teachers and students, money and food for the *Bauhaus* kitchen. He had to waste time in fighting attacks from German nationalists and reactionaries, from local craftsmen and circles close to the teaching staff of the former Academy of Fine Art. He had to use the utmost tact and much energy in keeping on good terms with Itten. Itten's influence was growing with teachers and students alike, and it created a monkish, Buddhist atmosphere at the *Bauhaus*.

In this situation a certain relief was provided for Gropius when the Grand Ducal Privy Purse, together with reactionary circles in the new administration, succeeded in dissolving again the union of the Academy of Fine Art and the School of Arts and Crafts which had formed the *Bauhaus*. On 4 April 1921 the Academy of Fine Art was re-opened as an independent institution, not under Gropius, but in the same building. The painters, Walther Klemm and Max Thedy, and the sculptor, Richard Engelmann, ceased to be *Bauhaus* teachers. Some students to whom Gropius' combination of art and the crafts was too materialistic, or Itten's artistic perception of inspiration and intuition too mystical, left also. However, the separation did not entirely clarify the *Bauhaus* position. This was only done through a "fifth column". Their pointed attacks forced Gropius to decide between Itten and himself.

In 1921 the Dutch painter and architect, Ch. E. M. Küpper, who called himself Theo van Doesburg, came to

Weimar, allegedly to accept an appointment as *Bauhaus* teacher, made by Gropius in 1919. Van Doesburg was the able and active representative of a group of Dutch artists, *De Stijl*, which had published a journal of the same name since 1917. The outlook of this group was conditioned by the work of the painter, Piet Mondrian, who created abstract compositions of straight lines and right angles, with the pure colours of red, blue and yellow, and tones of black, grey and white. The architects of the group, Jacob Johann Oud and Thomas Rietveld, accordingly worked mainly with cubes and planes at right angles. Actually Gropius had not appointed van Doesburg in 1919, nor did he appoint him in 1921 on his coming to Weimar. Then, in opposition to the *Bauhaus*, van Doesburg started a private training studio, right in the midst of the poor underfed *Bauhaus* students.

As work at the *Bauhaus* was then much determined by Itten and his followers among students and teachers, mainly Georg Muche and Lothar Schreyer, van Doesburg had no difficulty in identifying the whole school with the monkish-Buddhist-theosophical mood prevalent in the preliminary course and in some of the workshops. He publicly denounced the *Bauhaus* in his journal *De Stijl*. Rightly van Doesburg stated that Itten's preliminary course was not a suitable preparation for architecture, on the basis of a craft. In fact, Gropius' plan for a crafts training in preparation for creative work in architecture was alien to Itten. Itten's ideal was then the pious craftsman who – in mystical union with mineral, plant and animal matter – created individual objects. In this work certain devotional rites, meditation, breathing, diet, as well as clothes and housing of a certain type, were regarded as necessities. The result of all this was some opposition to Gropius, particularly from students of the preliminary course. They did not care to consider themselves "apprentices", and felt contempt for the kind of crafts training Gropius offered them. Instead they turned to dadaism and Schwitters' *Merz* art. With these discrepancies between Gropius' planned curriculum and the practical realities of Itten's, Muche's and Schreyer's teaching, van Doesburg's opposition had an easy task. The principles of *De Stijl* group allowed for a technical approach to architecture. Itten's preliminary course, if leading to architecture at all, would only tend towards buildings of symbolic meaning, harking back to, and perhaps exaggerating Antonio Gaudí's *Casa Milá* in Barcelona, of 1910.

In this light the rebellion of students like Gräff becomes understandable, as do Schlemmer's words in a letter of 23 June 1921.* As a *Bauhaus* teacher, he says, the title of a short story by Adalbert Stifter kept haunting him. It was

* Oskar Schlemmer, *Briefe und Tagebücher*. Munich 1958, p. 114

*Das Narrenschloss* – the Fools' Castle. The curiosity, typical for *Bauhaus* students, made a considerable number of them Doesburg's followers. With little foresight or understanding they were opposed to Itten and also to Gropius. In the spring of 1922 van Doesburg called together a congress of dadaists and constructivists in Weimar. Here a wide variety of opinions met, among them the Zurich dadaists, Hans Arp, Max Burchartz and Hans Richter, from Paris came the Roumanian dadaist, Tristan Tzara, and a confirmed representative of constructivism, El Lissitzky, came from the Soviet Union. From Hungary came the constructivists, Moholy-Nagy and Alfred Kemeny. Apart from van Doesburg himself, Cornelis van Eesteren represented the Dutch *Stijl* group. This congress had no tangible results, nor could it be expected to have any. The meeting brought together views of dadaists and constructivists who had nothing in common but their opposition to traditional art. To Gropius and the *Bauhaus* the congress was a nuisance as it added new if not better arguments to the internal opposition. Also, unfortunately, the *Bauhaus* itself made matters worse by staging in Weimar two exhibitions which strengthened the opposition of reactionary circles and constructivists. In April and May 1922 work of apprentices and "journeymen", mainly from Itten's preliminary course, was shown at the *Bauhaus*. Though Itten stressed in an exhibition leaflet that outsiders should not take either as playthings or finished work these exercises in material and structure of wood, glass, textiles, metal and paper, not few of the students looked at their own exercises as complete work, as complete as the work of the dadaists and Kurt Schwitters. The exhibition showed clearly a *l'art pour l'art* type of work in a dadaist vein, due to misunderstood studies of materials in the preliminary course. Itten himself was by no means free from futuristic and dadaist tendencies. This could be seen in his publication *Utopia*, with its typography in the style of the futurist journal *Lacerba*, and his experiments in reproducing the meaning of words like "Heaven", "Hell", or "Fear" pictorially, through the shape of their letters. This work was closely related to Hans Reimann's satire, *Literarisches Albdrücken*, of 1919, and tended to estrange students more and more from Gropius' idea of the crafts being the basis of creative art. The small exhibition of work from the preliminary course again made it easy for van Doesburg and his followers to point out mystical and romantic trends in the work of the *Bauhaus*. Quite unjustifiably they blamed Gropius for it. Van Doesburg and El Lissitzky did not understand Gropius' tolerant way of guiding people. The constructivists stood for order which, at the same time, meant submission to one way of thinking only.

The controversy about this exhibition remained limited chiefly to artists' circles, but a great public fuss was made on the occasion of the *Erste Thüringische Kunstausstellung*, in the summer of 1922, at the *Landesmuseum* in Weimar.

The Academy of Fine Art which had re-opened the previous year, presented itself to the public with the former *Bauhaus* teachers, Walther Klemm and Richard Engelmann, and the newly appointed graphic artists and painters, Alexander Olbricht, Felix Mesek and Hugo Gugg. Their work was shown in rooms at the right-hand side of the museum. Rooms on the left were occupied by independent work of the *Bauhaus* teachers, Lyonel Feininger, Johannes Itten, Paul Klee, Gerhard Marcks, Georg Muche and Lothar Schreyer. These were joined by young sympathisers, the Thuringian artists, Carl Crodel, Walter Dexel, Johannes Molzahn and Johannes Walter. This confrontation of abstract work from the *Bauhaus* teachers and their circle, with the conventional painting of the Academicians was very unwise. The work of the *Bauhaus* teachers was now seen by Weimar citizens, and the van Doesburg circle, to be closely related to the work they had previously seen from Itten's preliminary course, and this was judged to be the general standard of the *Bauhaus*. Political opponents came to the conclusion that at the *Bauhaus* young people were "misled by sick minds into useless activities". Followers of *De Stijl* in Weimar looked with contempt at paintings with other colours than red, blue and yellow, or shapes other than straight lines and segments of the circle. Gropius' most important plan of influencing the *Bauhaus* by outstanding but not dictatorial artistic personalities, both groups of opponents did not or would not understand.

The results of these two exhibitions, with the public at large and the *Bauhaus* internally, must have made Gropius realise that his ideas were in grave danger, in that he was not to be allowed time to develop them. Schlemmer's diaries and letters, the most important documents from a *Bauhaus* teacher, show clearly how Gropius' attitude changed at that time. In March 1922 Schlemmer still mentioned the wrong ideas the name of *Bauhaus* conjured up in the minds of the people who looked upon the *Bauhaus* workshops as places where artists played about and took up aesthetic attitudes. In June Schlemmer already wrote about: "Turning away from Utopia! We must be realistic, and strive for the realisation of ideas. Not cathedrals but machines to live in. Turning away from the Middle Ages and the medieval conception of the crafts and, in the end, from the crafts themselves practised only for training and for the sake of form."* At that moment design for industry was born, explained by Oskar Schlemmer in the very words Gropius had used in discussions with masters, "journeymen" and apprentices. Inside the *Bauhaus* Gropius was anxious to curb Itten's influence, in public he wished to demonstrate a greater sense of reality. Even in this difficult situation Gropius remained loyal to his idea of training the whole personality.

* Oskar Schlemmer, *Briefe und Tagebücher*. Munich 1958, pp. 124, 132

Though he wanted to break Itten's masterful influence, he did not want to replace one dogmatist by another, perhaps van Doesburg. The constructivists would certainly have been sympathetic to his plans for industrial and architectural design, but he would have had to sacrifice the creative activities of his friends, Adolf Meyer, Paul Klee, Lyonel Feininger and Gerhard Marcks, to van Doesburg's cold reasoning. Instead Gropius appointed a new member to the *Meisterrat* – the Masters' Council – a creative artist like the others, but possessing also remarkable educational talents. This new member was Wassily Kandinsky, a man who for years had held a leading position in twentieth-century art. Apart from his own creative work, the publication in 1912 of *Das Geistige in der Kunst* had helped him to become general superintendant of museums in the young Soviet Union, and lecturer at Moscow University.

With the appointment of Kandinsky Gropius combined re-arrangements in the workshops, designed mainly to limit Itten's influence and the sectarianism of the followers of Mazdaism, many of whom had become Beuron Pilgrims. Kandinsky became *Formmeister* for murals, Schlemmer for sculpture in stone and wood, Klee for stained glass, while Itten, assisted by Muche, remained in charge of the preliminary course and the metal workshop. Side by side there existed already, with Gropius' toleration, a kind of extra preliminary course described as "Study in Materials", unofficially taken by Joseph Albers, himself still an "apprentice". The pottery and weaving workshops remained unchanged. Backed by able technical masters and talented apprentices, they were doing good work. The other workshops, too, had improved with the help of skilled craftsmen, the sculptor, Josef Hartwig, the cabinet-maker, Weidensee, and the painter, Beberniss. Carl Zaubitzer and Lyonel Feininger worked together in the *Bauhaus* workshop for copper-plate printing and lithography. Through insufficient technical equipment the printing office did not have the status of a training workshop. The training of bookbinders had been given up, as it had proved impossible to equip a school workshop. Van de Velde's excellent bookbindery in the School of Arts and Crafts had, in 1915, become the private property of a master bookbinder, Otto Dorfner. This workshop, with Dorfner as technical master, would have made an excellent training ground, but Dorfner did not want to work with Klee as *Formmeister*. The connection of the school with Dorfner's workshop did not therefore last. This did not exclude the workshop from executing bindings for the *Bauhaus*, from designs by Klee and Feininger.

Kandinsky's appointment and the new arrangement of the workshops did much to reduce the influence of Itten and his followers. Van Doesburg's competitive opposition, however, grew stronger. He and his circle realised that through Kandinsky's appointment Gropius and the *Bauhaus* had gained in artistic stature. After the appointment, van Doesburg printed in *De Stijl* an article by Huszar. In it, as it were from abroad, the Thuringian State was blamed for committing a crime against civilisation by spending large sums of money on a project like Gropius' *Bauhaus*. Actually, Gropius had skilfully tried to appease the circle round van Doesburg and El Lissitzky through a further appointment. He had, however, carefully avoided asking either of the two men to co-operate personally. Instead he proposed to the Masters' Council the appointment of Laszlo Moholy-Nagy, Berlin editor of the Hungarian avant-garde journal *MA*. Moholy-Nagy had taken part in the Weimar congress of constructivists and dadaists, called by van Doesburg in 1922, and had worked in Berlin since 1921, actively and intelligently supported by his friend, Lucia, soon to become his wife. To begin with, Moholy-Nagy had great difficulties with the German language, and his early ideas on "Art and Society" were not given much attention in Germany, as they appeared in Hungarian in the journal *Ma*. Under the title "Constructivism and Proletariat" he wrote at that time: "In art the excitements of an age crystallize. Art is mirror and voice. The art of our time must be fundamental, precise and universal. Constructivism is this art. Constructivism is neither proletarian nor capitalistic. Constructivism is primeval ... Constructivism is visual socialism. This is our century: technology – machine – socialism. Come to terms with it, and shoulder the tasks of the century ..."* In his work as an artist Moholy-Nagy followed in the steps of Kasimir Malevich, the Russian precursor of constructivism. He also met El Lissitzky in Berlin, and became acquainted with his work. At an exhibition of Moholy-Nagy's work at the *Sturm* in Berlin, his three "Telephone Paintings" caused a minor sensation. With them he had tried to prove that constructivism could dispense with the personality of the artist in the execution of work. By telephone Moholy-Nagy had transmitted a diagram of shapes on graph paper, also colours tabulated by numbers, and specification of three different sizes, to a firm of enamel makers. As a result this firm had made three identical shape-and-colour constructions varying only in size. After that Moholy-Nagy was considered one of the most talented of the constructivists, free from prejudice, eager to learn, and brimful of ideas himself. Gropius' suggestion to appoint him to the *Bauhaus* seemed therefore an obvious choice. Constructivism, functioning as a link between technical and architectural work on the one side, and painting and sculpture on the other, was to be well received at the *Bauhaus*, specially when it was represented by an artist open to all tendencies, and not sworn to one dogma only. From the beginning Moholy-Nagy understood the relationship of creative design and industrial production. He arrived at the *Bauhaus*

* Sibyll Moholy-Nagy, *Laszlo Moholy-Nagy*. New York 1950, p. 35

in the spring of 1923, then twenty-eight years old. As a *Formmeister*, he took Itten's place who, soon after the limitations of his work imposed by the re-arrangements in the workshops at Kandinsky's appointment, had looked for a new occupation outside the *Bauhaus*, possibly in his native Switzerland. Moholy-Nagy took over the preliminary course, with the "Studies in Materials", started by the "apprentice" Joseph Albers, forming a transition stage, and later to become a continuation of the preliminary course. He also became *Formmeister* of the metal workshop which, under Itten, had produced jewellery of precious metals and devotional objects of high quality. Itten's leaving and the arrival of Moholy-Nagy were decisive moments in the life of the Weimar *Bauhaus*. Paul Citroen*, then an apprentice, openly confessed that the appointment was welcomed because constructivism was the very latest, and also because everybody hoped for differences between the young Moholy and the "old masters", Kandinsky, Klee and Feininger. This conflict, however, never came about. Gropius had been right in his expectations. "With the smiling enthusiasm of a child Moholy took on all tasks, and his vitality seemed unlimited" (Citroen). Moholy-Nagy saw the future importance of the *Bauhaus*, its tendencies and ideas. He learnt to appreciate Gropius' sound knowledge, his sure feeling for design, his tact and his gifts of diplomacy.

Moholy-Nagy had been appointed at the proper moment, for soon the *Bauhaus* was to be forced into a display much against Gropius' intention. It was again the question of a quick training being expected where Gropius intended slow developments. The Thuringian government demanded from Gropius that he should give an account of his work, by staging a large exhibition in the summer of 1923. The government acted under the pressure of political opposition by nationalistic and reactionary groups, also under the influence of local craftsmen. Last not least it listened to "The Voice from Abroad" represented by the Weimar circle round van Doesburg. Gropius had to agree, but it was not his wish to include a house in the *Bauhaus Ausstellung 1923*. In 1922 there did not yet exist a department of architecture. Buildings undertaken, for example *Haus Sommerfeld* in Berlin, *Haus Professor Dr. Auerbach* in Jena, and the alterations to the Jena Municipal Theatre, were works of Gropius' private office which was not a training ground for architects. According to Gropius' principles there could not exist a department of architecture in 1922, because a training including preliminary course, technical and art training, with an examination for "journeyman standard" at the end, would take three and a half years. If the autumn of 1919 is taken as the actual beginning of the *Bauhaus* work, the first "journeymen" could only have been ready

* Sibyll Moholy-Nagy, *Laszlo Moholy-Nagy*. New York 1950, p. 35

to start building in the summer term of 1923. As we have seen, Gropius did not mean the *Bauhaus* to provide a training for builders, rather was it to disseminate a new conception of artistic design.

In spite of all this, Gropius was pressed by the students to build the *Versuchshaus am Horn* for the 1923 exhibition. Students around the painter, Georg Muche, were keen to see his design for a one-family-house executed. The painters, Farkas Molnar and Walter Determann, were also busy designing houses for a *Bauhaus* settlement. The real enthusiasm for Muche's plan made Gropius give in. He did not comment on the design, but asked his office and his partner, Adolf Meyer, to collaborate on the execution. Most of the work on the interior was naturally left to the *Bauhaus* workshops, though there was also an obvious tendency for using mass-produced fittings for building and furnishings, as long as they were well designed. The workshops for wood, weaving, pottery, metal work and mural paintings designed the interior. For the first time that harmonious working together of many different personalities became obvious which was to be the hall-mark of the *Bauhaus*. The workshops had become efficient in the year since their re-arrangement. They had turned away from philosophising and dabbling in the arts and crafts, and had begun on a certain amount of designing for industry. They had also started using prefabricated materials. The achievement of the wood-working shop was impressive. There were Dickmann's desk and chair, and Marcel Breuer's chair with strapped woven seat, immediate forerunner of his tubular steel chair of 1925. These, as well as Breuer's nursery furniture, made with plywood, and other pieces made for the experimental house, hinted at a revolution in design, later to spread from the *Bauhaus*. Peter Keler's cradle, built according to Kandinsky's theory of colour, of blue circles, yellow triangles and red squares, was a delightful example of trying to combine theories of colour and shape, learnt at the *Bauhaus*, with the practical work of the craftsman.

The *Formmeister* at the weaving workshop, Georg Muche, had changed after Itten's leaving Weimar, and was getting closer to Gropius' ideas of work and training. These ideas did not aim at just creating woven pictures as works of art. The gathering of technical experience, necessary for quality work in designing for industry, was of equal importance. Textiles, designed as material to be sold by the yard, were used in the experimental house, and the wood-working shop had at its disposal for upholstery materials from the weaving workshop. Thanks to the steadiness of Gerhard Marcks and Max Krehan, and the great gifts of the "journeymen" Otto Lindig and Theo Bogler, the Dornburg pottery had succeeded in making contacts with industry. This enabled the workshop to supply the experimental house with china from the Volkstedt and Berlin porcelain manufactures, made from *Bauhaus* designs.

The workshops for mural painting, sculpture and stained glass planned to show their work mainly in the school itself and in the workshops. The title of Gropius' lecture, "Art and Technics, a new Unity", could serve as a programme for the exhibition. When, in the summer of 1922, Schlemmer had spoken about "turning away from Utopia" and "machines to live in instead of cathedrals", he had hinted at these developments. We can only guess how Gropius managed to come to terms with independent artists like Feininger, Kandinsky, Klee and Marcks, concerning his new aims which put technics into the place of the crafts. A programme which regarded art and technics as a new unity, must have been alien to them. To themselves and probably also to many students they appeared no longer wanted. Later Gropius defined the function of these artists as continuing to develop their own work, within the frame of the *Bauhaus*, and by doing so creating the kind of atmosphere, essential for a school of design. When Gropius prepared the *Bauhaus* exhibition, it must have been his personality which encouraged the independent artists to stay with the *Bauhaus*. "I pity the man who is not uplifted, in some way or other, by him (Gropius)," Feininger wrote to his wife, shortly before the exhibition opened.*

The exhibition took place between 15 August and 30 September 1923. It took in the *Versuchshaus am Horn*, and the entrances, halls and stairways of the school building where the workshops for murals, stained glass and sculpture exhibited. In the workshops themselves and in the schoolrooms individual work – from the workshops – was shown, as well as examples demonstrating the nature of the preliminary course. Individual work – outside school training – was shown by "masters" and "journeymen" in the *Staatliches Landesmuseum*. Of special importance was that part of the exhibition arranged by Gropius and Meyer. By displaying designs, drawings, photos and models on the theme "International Architecture", it tried to show that the new way of building was neither an invention of *De Stijl* or Soviet Russia, nor was it an eccentric notion of Gropius himself. It was a concern of all Europe. Here Gropius' ideas about the house of the future were displayed, when he showed models of houses, designed in co-operation with Meyer, to be erected from prefabricated units. They could be varied by different assembly.

A *Bauhaus* week, from 15 to 19 August, opened the project. Gropius' lecture on "Art and Technics" was followed by talks from Oud and Kandinsky, a performance of Schlemmer's "Triadic Ballet", and a *Bauhaus* "mechanistic cabaret". There were also shows of scientific slow-motion pictures, then in their infancy. The musical performances were particularly brilliant, and included the first night of Hindemith's composition of Rilke's *Marien-*

* Hans Maria Wingler, *Das Bauhaus*. Bramsche 1963, p. 83

*lieder*, the original performance of six compositions for piano by Feruccio Busoni, a performance of Křenek's *Concerto grosso*, with Hermann Scherchen conducting, and the second performance, in Germany, of Stravinsky's *L'Histoire du Soldat*. Stravinsky travelled from Paris to Weimar, to be present, and always remembered the occasion because at Weimar he came to know and respect Busoni. Till then he had considered him an over-severe critic.

The exhibition in the *Landesmuseum* brought together work by Joseph Albers, Herbert Bayer, Marcel Breuer, Paul Citroen, Lyonel Feininger, Ludwig Hirschfeld, Johannes Itten, Wassily Kandinsky, Paul Klee, Gerhard Marcks, Laszlo Moholy-Nagy, Georg Muche, Hinnerk Scheper, Oskar Schlemmer, Lothar Schreyer, Joost Schmidt and others. No other country or city in the Old or New World can boast of having staged, only five years after the First World War, a cultural event of such quality. Only few realised in the summer of 1923, how Gropius and his *Bauhaus* community had turned an exhibition, forced on them prematurely, into an outstanding success.

Moholy-Nagy gave Gropius most valuable assistance in preparing and carrying through the project. Publicity material, posters and lettering, all showed the strong influence of a functionalism which Moholy-Nagy's constructivist tendencies had introduced to the *Bauhaus*. Some publicity material was designed by him, other designs came from Schlemmer, Bayer and Schmidt. It was due to Moholy's example and encouragement that publicity and lettering, as well as general décor, no longer showed the futuristic influence, too obvious in the programme leaflets of the *Bauhaus-Abende* two years before. In general, the *Bauhaus* now followed Moholy-Nagy's maxim: "Typography must convey a clear message in the most impressive manner." A great advance was the choice for most of the material of a fat Roman type, oddly called *Grotesk* by the printers. Its use in posters and signs by the students, Peter Keler, Farkas Molnar, Herbert Bayer and Joseph Maltan, might even now, after more than forty years, serve as a model for traffic signs. At Moholy-Nagy's suggestion the book, *Staatliches Bauhaus in Weimar 1919–1923*, a documentation of the exhibition, was designed. With binding by Herbert Bayer, layout by Moholy-Nagy, text by Gropius, Klee, Kandinsky, Grunow, Moholy-Nagy and Schlemmer, and original lithographs by Hirschfeld-Mack, Breuer, Bayer and Keler, the book was a landmark in book production. For bookwork the *Bauhaus* had to rely on outside printing, as the school-owned hand-press was only suited to pictorial work in lithography, relief printing or intaglio from a wood-block or copperplate. Under Feininger's direction this press produced the four folders of *Bauhausdrucke*, the folder of 1923, with works by the *Bauhaus* masters, a folder of twelve woodcuts by Feininger, Kandinsky's *Kleine Welten*, a folder, *Italia*, with 12 lithographs by Farkas Molnar and H. Stefan, and Gerhard Marcks' woodcuts for "Wieland's Song" from the *Edda*. It is characteristic of the *Bauhaus* spirit that these works by independent artists, though reproductions, were not influenced by the new emphasis on "technics". Feininger's exquisite title-pages, tables of contents and imprints, in lithography, for the four folders of *Bauhausdrucke* show no break, though some were produced before and some after the changes in the *Bauhaus*. This "Lettering as Art" is evident also in all Feininger's written letters, and became part of the whole creative atmosphere. Herbert Bayer's typeface, *Universal*, or Joseph Albers' letters for stencilling, of 1925, are closer to Feininger's title-pages than these title-pages are to the lettering of futurists and dadaists. Lettering, expressing artistic individuality and clarity at the same time, is typical of what *Bauhaus* design came to mean. Klee's *Pädagogisches Skizzenbuch*, though published only after the Weimar period, is an excellent example of the combination of artistic freedom and clear presentation. In it Moholy-Nagy clarified Klee's highly individualistic informative sketches. He lent them the significance of formulae in a book of mathematics, at the same time preserving their special character.

During the Weimar exhibition the new *Bauhaus* typography received attention through orders for mass production. The Thuringian State commissioned bank-notes in denominations of one and two million and one milliard marks from Herbert Bayer's design. These notes were issued on 9 August 1923. At the beginning of the exhibition half a dollar was worth one million marks, and when the exhibition closed it was worth eighty million marks.

Among the crafts Moholy-Nagy preferred working with glass. Soon after he had taken over the metal workshop, he included glass in its production, and stimulated experiments for combining the two in electric light fittings. Instead of hand-wrought seven-armed candelabras, apprentices of the metal workshop now made the first globe-shaped lamps of glass and metal. Instead of making hand-beaten samovars, they now experimented with tea pots and tea infusers of many kinds which proved good models for mass production.

The winter term – 1923/24 – after the exhibition, became the most successful period of the Weimar years. All the workshops developed a clear conception of industrial design. It was then that Gropius' idea of appointing independent artists as *Formmeister*, and thereby influencing the whole personality of the student, bore its first fruit. Even just shortly before the exhibition there had been adverse comments from disgruntled "journeymen" and apprentices, followed by direct requests for the dismissal of the "merely decorative" prestige masters, such as Kandinsky and Klee, to improve the lot of the "journeymen". After the exhibition, however, all criticism stopped and

Gropius was proved right. In growing numbers "journeymen" developed into personalities. Albers, Bayer, Breuer, Scheper, Lindig, Molnar and Gunta Stölzl, all had now obtained full mastery of their craft, both from the point of view of design and technique. With their help, Gropius was ready to include the teaching of architecture in the *Bauhaus* curriculum. Misunderstandings which had arisen through the name *Bauhaus*, and Gropius' new ways of "Art and Technics", began to clear away. The question of a unity of art and technics, and technics and crafts on a higher level was now discussed. Schlemmer wrote in his diary, under 18 March 1924, concerning the future possibilities of the *Bauhaus*: "The roads are dividing. New theories of construction demand immediate use ... Design of objects for daily use, and even more so for houses themselves, with everything in them must be reconsidered ... 'Absolute art', 'pure' form and colour are part of architecture and of everything inside a building. Painting needs a connection with the physical world. Its finest object: man. Does that rehabilitate the ancient theory of aesthetics? I believe it does. Some principles seem unshakable and eternally new. They may appear again and again in a new guise, and that is as it should be. New, proud and great tasks."*

A happy creative atmosphere filled the *Bauhaus* at the beginning of 1924, and progress was good. Also, with the stabilising of the German currency, it was possible, for the first time in years, to plan with some certainty. Nevertheless, when Schlemmer made his diary entries, in March 1924, the fate of the *Bauhaus* was already in the balance. Elections for the Thuringian *Landtag* had swept away the parliamentary socialist majority, and brought in a government of the right. Conservatives and reactionaries who had previously opposed the *Bauhaus*, gained power in the administration of the country. Together with jealous Weimar craftsmen, they were now in a strong position to attack Gropius and his "Cathedral of Socialism". New work in architecture and design for industry immediately suffered. *Bauhaus* "journeymen" and "young masters" faced insecurity through its possible closing. However, the untiring zeal of Gropius offered a compromise which appeared to be acceptable to a parliamentary majority of the Thuringian *Landtag*. To reduce costs, he suggested turning the workshops over to commercial production. By producing goods and later on licensing designs for industry, they would keep themselves. In future the State would be responsible only for the school building and a small staff. Not all *Bauhaus* masters liked this plan. They feared that production in the workshops might take first place. Gerhard Marcks wrote to Gropius from the Dornburg pottery: "We must always keep in mind that the *Bauhaus* is meant to be a training ground ...

* Oskar Schlemmer, *Briefe und Tagebücher*. Munich 1958, p.161

Production must never be the aim, or the *Bauhaus* will become factory No. 101– of which a hundred exist already, in other words, a completely indifferent institution."* There was also the question of what would become of those workshops which had no chance in commercial production: Schlemmer's stagecraft, Kandinsky's mural painting and Klee's stained glass. Gropius himself did not know the answer. He wanted to gain time, time for work, time for letting a public opinion settle which was becoming sympathetic to new trends in design. Given this time, there was justified hope that the commercial success of the workshops for architecture, woodwork, metal work, weaving and pottery would keep the *Bauhaus* going as a whole. However, Gropius was not allowed this breathing space in Weimar. In September 1924 the Thuringian Ministry of Education gave "cautionary" notice, for March 1925, to all teachers and employees of the *Bauhaus*.

A flood of public protest resulted from this measure. The daily papers, with the exception of the nationalistic and reactionary ones, joined in. Architects drew attention, in their professional journals, to the significance of this new experiment. Even the worst of the former opponents, the artists round van Doesburg and *De Stijl*, relented because they did not want to find themselves in line with a reactionary opposition. Not so long before they had furiously attacked the "renegade" Moholy-Nagy for supporting the cause of Gropius. In their new journal *G*, edited by El Lissitzky, Hans Richter and Werner Gräff, there appeared in June 1924 an editorial, declaring conformity with the *Bauhaus*' new ideology. Former attacks, this notice stated, had been aimed solely at "the inadequacy of certain people and methods". Very serious though equally vain protest came from a "Circle of Friends of the *Bauhaus*", formed in the spring of 1924. It made no difference, though the governing body of the Circle included such personalities of European reputation as the architects, Behrens, Poelzig, Berlage and Hoffmann, the painters, Chagall and Kokoschka, the musicians, Adolf Busch, Edwin Fischer and Arnold Schönberg, the writers, Gerhart Hauptmann, Franz Werfel and Herbert Eulenberg, as well as the scholars, Albert Einstein and Joseph Strzygowsky.

It is true, negotiations continued after notices had been served, but they were continued by the opposition mainly to force Gropius into taking a step which would justify to the public the closing down of the *Bauhaus*. The government achieved its aim when after a conducted tour of the *Bauhaus*, taken by the whole Ministry, on 23 December 1924, Gropius was told that the only possibility now was signing new contracts with six-monthly notice. As a reply

* Annegret Janda, *Bauhaus-Keramik. Kunstmuseen der DDR.* Vol. II, 1959, p. 90

to this unreasonable suggestion, which did not allow for continuous work at the school, Gropius and the *Form-meister* published, three days later, on 26 December 1924, a declaration of the closing down of the *Bauhaus* in Weimar, as from 31 March 1925, when their contracts would come to an end. The government accepted this declaration, though a state institution could not actually be dissolved by a director and staff under notice. The satisfaction of reactionary circles, the relief of having no longer to deal with the unexpectedly broad front of advocates for the *Bauhaus*, made the Thuringian government ignore such scruples in closing the school. With an imposing letter of protest to the Thuringian government, of 13 January, the whole *Bauhaus* community, students, "journeymen", and apprentices, made it clear that they agreed with the steps their masters had taken.* They were in complete sympathy, and together with their masters they wanted to leave the disrupted institution, to continue their common work somewhere else.

This protest made the most obstinate opponents realise what the *Bauhaus* – now being driven out of Weimar – had come to mean. It had succeeded in five years of work in achieving agreement on the essential questions of design, as was shown in its production.

The very foundations Gropius had considered necessary, were laid. The dual function of *Formmeister* and technical master was now united in the *Jungmeister*, fully trained to solve questions of design and techniques.

The following three months of 1925 were to provide the answer to the question whether the *Bauhaus* was an art school like others, or a new far-reaching experiment for training people in a new conception of art and design. Other art colleges tried to get some of the *Bauhaus* masters for their own staff, and in Weimar a plan emerged for some sort of continuation of the school, without Gropius, Moholy-Nagy, Klee, Kandinsky, Schlemmer, Feininger and Muche, but with workshops and a department of architecture under the architect, Otto Bartning. Feininger was told of the possibility of a professorship at the Weimar Academy of Fine Art, with the existing staff of Klemm, Mesek, Olbricht and Engelmann. Apart from Gerhard Marcks who accepted an appointment to the art school in Halle-Giebichenstein, and one or two technical masters, the *Bauhaus* community waited together to see whether and where there might occur a new possibility.

Soon this problem was to be solved. On 1 April 1925 the *Bauhaus*, masters and students, with few exceptions, moved to Dessau. Only then did it become obvious what amazing spade work had been done in Weimar. The

* Hans Maria Wingler, *Das Bauhaus*. Bramsche 1963, p. 106

"young masters", Joseph Albers, Herbert Bayer, Marcel Breuer, Hinnerk Scheper, Joost Schmidt and Gunta Stölzl, together with Gropius, Klee, Kandinsky, Moholy-Nagy, Muche and Schlemmer now transplanted the *Bauhaus* idea to Dessau. After a short time the re-opened *Bauhaus* workshops were able to supply, in the field of wood, metal, colour, textiles, printing, and advertising, dozens of models for industry. Gropius immediately found himself with an exciting project. The town passed the erection of a block of buildings to form the new *Bauhaus*. Also Gropius' and Meyer's advanced ideas on architecture could now be put to the test when three semi-detached houses, and one detached house were to be built for members of the teaching staff. The Weimar exhibition of 1923 had shown models of prefabricated houses of the same basic type, varying only in the different assembly of their separate units. Now these houses were actually to be put up. Fundamental agreement on questions of design the *Bauhaus* community had brought with them to their new home.

A backward glance at the workshop production in Weimar shows clearly how the *Bauhaus* conception of design developed. At the new start this concept made itself felt in a wide variety of things made, ranging from a humble ashtray to the school building and houses of the staff.

In the early designs for layout and lettering, Peter Röhl followed expressionism, while Friedl Dicker was influenced by dadaism, and Johannes Itten by futurism. The unknown artist of the lithographed sheet for the *Richtfest of Haus Sommerfeld*, 1920, appears to have been guided by Rudolf Koch's typography, the Gothic type and the style of the German *Wandervogel* movement. Only three years later Moholy-Nagy's maxim that "typography must convey a clear message" became generally accepted at the *Bauhaus*. Oskar Schlemmer's publicity leaflet for the *Bauhaus* exhibition of 1923 is a perfect example of early work. Moholy-Nagy's design for the cover of *Idee und Aufbau*, with its composition of straight lines and segments of the circle, is in contrast completely austere. The "clear message" on Bayer's bank-notes is a model of what one would still like to see on bank-notes and coins.

Textile work started with woven "pictures", painted, as it were, not with paints and brush, but with coloured threads. Towards the end of the Weimar period, however, there appeared designs for fabrics, and experiments with various types of textiles led to using these pleasing combinations as models for mass production. The general agreement on questions of design appears clearly in a layout by Schlemmer, and a textile picture by Suse Ackermann.

For furniture it is sufficient to compare Marcel Breuer's black chair, with coloured woven straps, nice to look at but painful to sit on, with his easy chair, made of broad strips of wood and narrow straps. If the black chair fitted in only with the round black table, on five stout legs, the easy chair goes equally well with Rosen's secretaire, or Dickmann's desk.

Experiments in design of the metal workshop as, for example, the jug by Martin Jahn, and a tall liqueur bottle by Julius Pap, were followed, under Moholy-Nagy's direction, by Marianne Brandt's jugs and bowls which, true to theory, were designed essentially from sections of the globe, and flat surfaces. The inclusion of glass in the metal workshop led to the excellent early glass-and-metal table lamp by Jucker and Wilhelm Wagenfeld. *Bauhaus* work on the combination of glass and metal was the first step towards a revolution in the design of light fittings and kitchen utensils. This work was continued by the *Bauhaus* at Dessau, and the *Staatliche Bauhochschule* in Weimar. The pottery of the *Bauhaus* showed in the beginning the remains of folk-art tradition, combined with expressionistic design. But as the *Formmeister*, Gerhard Marcks, and the master pupil, Otto Lindig, were both born sculptors, the production of their workshop escaped the teething troubles of painted underglaze. Instead, there were experiments in shape where the sculptor gained the upper hand over the potter. It is pleasant to see how soon these potters strove towards perfection, with a material not in need of glazing. Objects then had firm outlines, with distinct parts, foot, body and neck, and obtruding lips, very different from the approximation of shape of peasant-pottery tradition. As true sculptors the *Bauhaus* potters stressed the beauty of the material itself.

The *Bauhaus* pottery had started supplying models for industry at the end of the Weimar period. As the pottery did not move to Dessau, this *Bauhaus* tradition did not continue in direct line. But Otto Lindig became its noted exponent when he took over the Dornburg pottery, where he carried on his own production and the training of apprentices till well into the dark thirties.

We have seen then that under Gropius there evolved a community of creative artists, which after moving to Dessau and re-establishing the workshops, consolidated its contacts for providing design and models for industry. It was to the advantage of the *Bauhaus* community that the German inflation was followed, between 1924–1929, by a period of prosperity. Building activity increased, and with this key industry increased the kind of production of particular interest to *Bauhaus* designers. In this way, the small group of artists, which came together in Weimar in 1919, following Gropius' appeal, had become exponents of his theory of a responsible training for designers. The Weimar *Bauhaus* under Gropius, assisted above all by Moholy-Nagy, contributed greatly to the emergence of industrial design. It helped to bring to the attention of those in charge of industry the need for thinking in terms of men and not mechanism.

# plates

The respective numbers following the captions refer to the consecutive numbers of the List of Plates.

Peter Röhl. Publicity leaflet
for the "Bauhaus-Abende" *(1)*

Friedl Dicker. Programme
for the first "Bauhaus-Abend",
14.4.1920 *(2)*

**ANALYSEN ALTER MEISTER**

JOHANNES ITTEN

DIE FURCHT DES HERRN IST ANFANG ALLER ER-KENNTNIS. DIE RUCHLOSEN VERACHTEN WEISHEIT UND ZUCHT

⟨Sprüche Salomonis I, 7⟩

WER DA EIN HERZ HAT, DER WERFE DAS AUGE WEG, DANN WIRD ER SCHAUEN.

⟨Hussain al Hallâdsch⟩

„Denken heisst wiedererinnern"       (PLATO)

Schaffen heisst wiedererschaffen.
Geboren werden heisst wiedergeboren werden.

Denn Gott schuf die Prinzipien aller Dinge,

alles Geschaffenen von

Anbeginn

an.

Johannes Itten and Friedl Dicker.
Text page from the yearbook
"Utopia" (6)

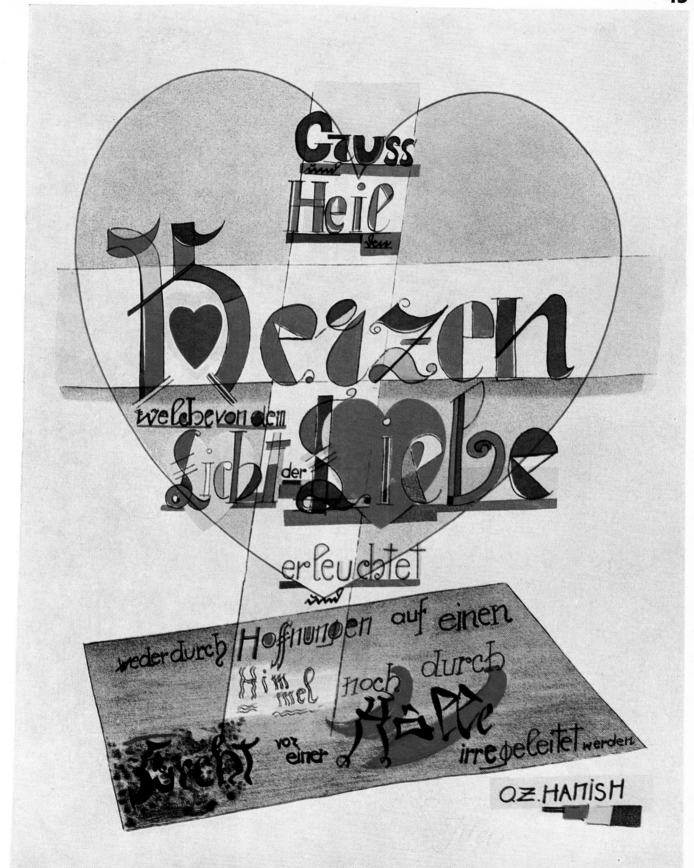

Johannes Itten.
"Spruch"
(Bauhaus folder I/3) (8)

Farkas Molnar and H. Stefan. Title-page of the folder "Italia" (5)

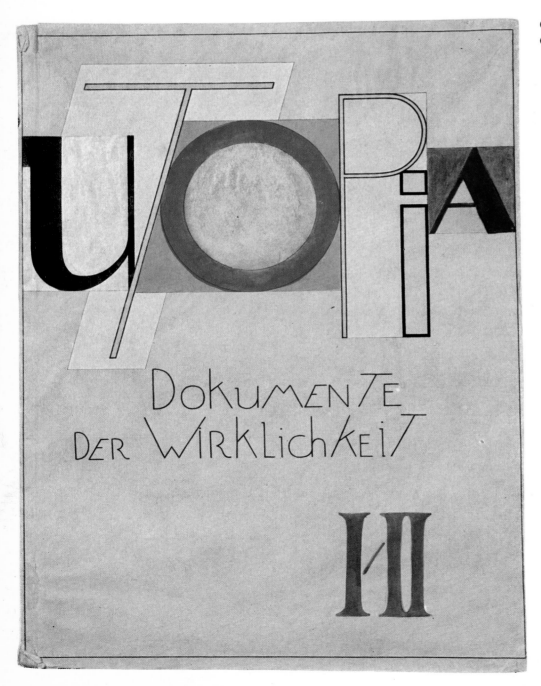

Oskar Schlemmer.
Cover of the yearbook "Utopia" (7)

Lyonel Feininger.
Title-page of Bauhaus folder I (9)

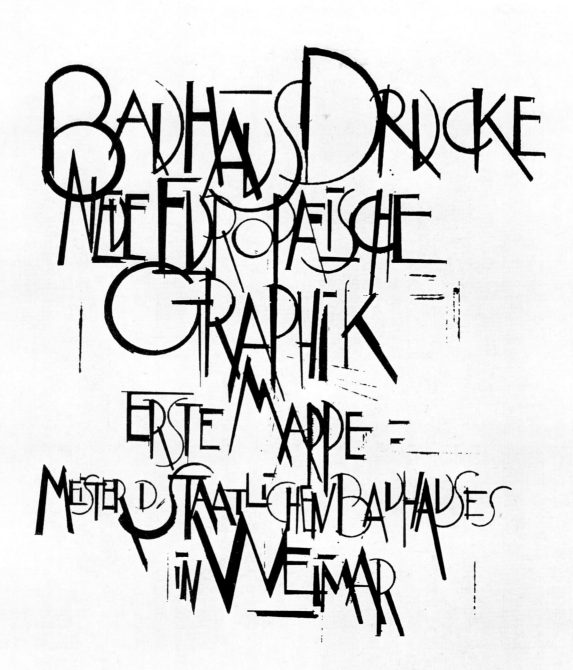

BAUHAUS DRUCKE
NEUE EUROPAEISCHE
GRAPHIK
ERSTE MAPPE
MEISTER D. STAATLICHEN BAUHAUSES
IN WEIMAR

HERGESTELLT UND HERAUSGEGEBEN VOM STAATLICHEN BAUHAUS IN WEIMAR IM JAHRE 1921 ZU BEZIEHEN DURCH MÜLLER & CO VERLAG POTSDAM

Oskar Schlemmer.

DIE
ERSTE
BAUHAUS-
AUSSTELLUNG
IN WEIMAR
JULI BIS SEPTEMBER
1923

DAS STAATLICHE BAUHAUS

LEITUNG
WALTER GROPIUS

SYNDIKUS
EMIL LANGE

LEHRENDE MEISTER
FÜR DIE FORMLEHRE
LYONEL FEININGER, WALTER GROPIUS, JOHANNES ITTEN
WASSILY KANDINSKY, PAUL KLEE, GERHARD MARCKS
GEORG MUCHE, OSKAR SCHLEMMER, LOTHAR SCHREYER
GERTRUD GRUNOW, ADOLF MEYER
FÜR DIE WERKLEHRE
HEINRICH BEBERNISS, HELENE BÖRNER, CHRISTIAN DELL
ANTON HANDIK, JOSEF HARTWIG, MAX KREHAN
EMIL LANGE, CARL ZAUBITZER

Publicity leaflet for the 1923 exhibition *(13)*

## DAS STAATLICHE BAUHAUS

ist die erste und bisher einzige staatliche Schule des Reichs — wenn nicht der Welt — welche die schöpferischen Kräfte bildender Kunst aufruft zu wirken während sie lebendig sind und zugleich mit der Errichtung von Werkstätten auf handwerklicher Grundlage deren Verbindung und fruchtbare Durchdringung erstrebt mit dem Ziel der Vereinigung im Bau. Der Baugedanke soll die verlorene Einheit wiederbringen, die in einem versackten Akademikertum und einem verbosselten Kunstgewerbe zugrunde ging; er soll die grosse Beziehung aufs Ganze wiederherstellen und in einem höchsten Sinn das Gesamtkunstwerk ermöglichen. Das Ideal ist alt, seine Fassung jedoch immer wieder neu; die Erfüllung ist der Stil und nie war der Wille zum Stil mächtiger als eben heute. Aber die Verwirrung der Geister und Begriffe macht, dass Kampf und Streit um sein Wesen ist, das aus dem Zusammenprall der Ideen heraus sich bilden wird als die neue Schönheit. — Eine solche Schule, bewegend und in sich selbst bewegt, wird ungewollt zum Gradmesser der Erschütterungen des politischen und geistigen Lebens der Zeit und die Geschichte des Bauhauses wird zur Geschichte gegenwärtiger Kunst.

Das Staatliche Bauhaus, gegründet nach der Katastrophe des Kriegs, im Chaos der Revolution und zur Zeit der Hochblüte einer gefühlsgeladenen explosiven Kunst, wird zunächst zum Sammelpunkt derer, die zukunftsgläubig-himmelstürmend die Kathedrale des Sozialismus bauen wollen. Die Triumphe von Industrie und Technik vor dem Krieg und deren Orgie im Zeichen der Vernichtung währenddessen, riefen jene leidenschaftliche Romantik wach, die flammende Protest war gegen Materialismus und Mechanisierung von Kunst und Leben. Die Not der Zeit war auch die Not der Geister. Ein Kult des Unbewussten, Undeutbaren, ein Hang zu Mystik und Sektiererei entsprang dem Suchen nach den letzten Dingen, die in einer Welt voll Zweifel und Zerrissenheit um ihren Sinn gebracht zu werden drohten. Der Durchbruch der Bezirke klassischer Ästhetik verstärkte die Grenzenlosigkeit des Fühlens, die in der Entdeckung des Ostens und der Künste der Neger, Bauern, Kinder und Irren Nahrung oder Bestätigung fand. Der Ursprung künstlerischen Schaffens wurde ebenso gesucht wie seine Grenzen kühn erweitert. Eine Inbrunst der Ausdrucksmittel entstand wie auf den Bildern der Altäre. Doch Bilder und immer wieder Bilder sind es, in die sich die entscheidungsvollen Werte flüchten. Als Höchstleistungen individueller Übersteigerung, fessellos und unerlöst zugleich, mussten sie der proklamierten Synthese, ausser der Einheit des Bildes selbst, alles schuldig bleiben. — Das biedere Handwerk tummelt sich in exotischer Lust am Stoffe und die Baukunst türmt Utopien auf Papier.

Die Umkehrung der Werte, Wechsel von Standpunkt, Name und Begriff ergibt das Gegenbild, den nächsten Glauben. Dada, Hofnarr in diesem Reiche, spielt Ball mit Paradoxen und macht die Atmosphäre frei und leicht. Amerikanismus auf Europa übertragen, die neue in die alte Welt gekellt, Tod der Vergangenheit, dem Mondschein und der Seele, so schreitet die neue Welt. Vernunft und Wissenschaft „des Menschen allerhöchste Kraft" sind die Regenten und der Ingenieur ist der gelassene Vollstrecker der unbegrenzten Möglichkeiten. Mathematik, Konstruktion und Mechanismus sind die Elemente und Macht und Geld die Diktatoren der modernen Phänomene aus Eisen, Beton, Glas, Elektrizität. Geschwindigkeit des Starren, Entmaterialisierung der Materie, Organisation des Unorganischen erzeugen Wunder der Abstraktion. Gegründet auf Naturgesetze sind sie das Werk des Geistes zur Bezwingung der Natur, gegründet auf die Macht des Kapitals ein Werk des Menschen gegen Menschen. Tempo und Hochspannung des Merkantilen machen Zweck und Nutzen zum Maßstab aller Wirkung und die Berechnung ergreift die transzendente Welt: die Kunst ein Logarithmus. Sie, ihres Namens längst beraubt, lebt ein Leben nach dem Tode, im Monument des Würfels und im Farbquadrat. Religion ist der präzise Denkprozess und Gott ist tot. Der Mensch, der Selbstbewusste und Vollkommene, von jeder Puppe an Exaktheit übertroffen, harrt auf die Resultate der Retorten, bis sich die Formel auch für „Geist" gefunden . . . . . .

Goethe: „Wenn die Hoffnungen sich verwirklichen, dass die Menschen sich mit allen ihren Kräften, mit Herz und Geist, mit Verstand und Liebe sich vereinigen und voneinander Kenntnis nehmen, so wird sich ereignen, woran jetzt noch kein Mensch denken kann — Allah braucht nicht mehr zu schaffen, wir erschaffen seine Welt." Es ist die Synthese, die Zusammenfassung, Steigerung und Verdichtung alles Positiven zur starken Mitte. Die Idee der Mitte, fern von Halbheit und Schwäche, verstanden als Wage und Gleichgewicht wird zur Idee der deutschen Kunst. Deutschland, Land der Mitte, und Weimar, Herz in diesem, ist nicht zum ersten Mal Wahlstatt geistiger Entscheidung. Es geht um die Erkenntnis dessen, was uns gemäss ist, um uns nicht ziellos zu verlieren, im Ausgleich der polaren Gegensätze; fernste Vergangenheit wie fernste Zukunft liebend; Reaktion wie Anarchismus abgewandt; vom Selbstzweck, Einzel-Ich im Anmarsch auf das Typische, vom Problematischen zum Gültigen und Festen — so werden wir zu Trägern der Verantwortung und zum Gewissen der Welt. Ein Idealismus der Aktivität, der Kunst und Wissenschaft und Technik umfasst, durchdringt und einigt und in der Forschung — Lehre — Arbeit wirkt, wird den Kunst-Bau des Menschen aufführen, der zu dem Weltgebäude nur ein Gleichnis ist. Wir können heute nicht mehr tun, als den Plan des Ganzen zu bedenken, Grund zu legen und die Bausteine zu bereiten. Aber WIR SIND! WIR WOLLEN! UND WIR SCHAFFEN!

## IN WEIMAR

## DIE AUSSTELLUNG 1923

| | | |
|---|---|---|
| **DIE SCHULE** | zeigt Erziehung und Bildung des Menschen auf dem Wege von Handwerk und Kunst. Die Schule will den bildnerisch Begabten aus dem naiven Basteln und Werken zu der Erkenntnis seiner Mittel und ihrer Gesetze und daraus zur Freiheit schöpferischen Gestaltens führen. An Schulbeispielen solcher Art mit besonderer Einstellung auf das Werkmässige werden Lehrgänge gezeigt, die von programmatischer Bedeutung für den Kunstunterricht sind. | AUSSTELLUNG VON NATUR-STUDIEN FORM- FARB- UND MATERIE-STUDIEN MATERIALKOMPOSITIONEN |
| **DIE WERK-STÄTTEN** | zeigen selbständige und auf den Bau bezogene Werkarbeit der Tischlerei, Holz- und Steinbildhauerei, Wandmalerei, Glas- und Metallwerkstätten, Töpferei und Weberei. Die Kenntnis des Materials, seine Gesetze und Möglichkeiten, die Durchdringung der Handwerklichen und Formalen (künstlerische Phantasie) soll aus dem Zusammenbruch des zunftmässigen Werkens von einst und geistloser Maschinenarbeit von heute jene Synthese herstellen, die ein Gebilde schön, neu und zweckmässig macht. Auf dem Wege solcher Gestaltung ist das Handwerk im alten Sinne heute Uebergang, das die vollendete Maschine nicht ausschliesst, sondern erstrebt. Die Ueberleitung der Schulwerkstätten in produktive ist eine Frage aber auch ein Gebot der Zeit. | AUSSTELLUNG VON EINZELERZEUGNISSEN DER WERKSTÄTTEN FÜR STEIN, HOLZ, METALL, TON, GLAS, FARBE, GEWEBE |
| **DER BAU** | zeigt das einfache Haus und seine Einrichtung. Denn Sinn und Wesen der Bauhausarbeit ist der Bau und unser unmittelbares Ziel die Gestaltung unserer Wohnstätte nach den Bedürfnissen und Möglichkeiten heutigen Lebens. Der Zusammenschluss alles werkmässigen Gestaltens im Dienste einer Idee, die Bau- und Hausidee, die Zweckbeziehung und Bindung aller Teile macht kollektive Arbeit zur Notwendigkeit und damit den Bau zum Gemeinschaftswerk. Das Siedlungsgelände des Bauhauses soll einem weitgefassten Siedlungsplan dienen, der Einzelhäuser, Bad, Spielplatz und Gärten umfasst. Das weitgesteckte Ziel des Bauhauses schliesst den metaphysischen Bau nicht aus, der über die Schönheit des Zweckvollen hinaus als wahrhaftes Gesamtkunstwerk die Verwirklichung einer abstrakten monumentalen Schönheit erstrebt. | EIN HAUS UND SEINE EINRICHTUNG SIEDLUNGSPLÄNE UND HAUSMODELLE UTOPISCHES AUSSTELLUNG INTERNATIONALER ARCHITEKTEN |
| **MALEREI UND PLASTIK** | zeigen Einzelwerke und ihre Vereinigung und Bindung durch Architektur. Die Aufgabe der bildenden Kunst war zu allen Zeiten grossen Stils eine ethische und sie wird es fernerhin sein. Stoff und Ideen der Darstellung haben sich gewandelt ebenso wie ihre Darstellungsmittel. Mit der Heraufkunft einer neuen Baukunst ist die monumentale Kunst heute wieder im Werden, vorweggenommen oder vorbereitet im Einzelbild, das sich von architektonischen Vorstellungen leiten lässt oder auch über jegliche Beziehung sich hinwegsetzt. Solche Unabhängigkeit schafft ihm weitesten Spielraum und lässt es die Grenzen bildnerischen Gestaltens kühn erweitern. | INTERNATIONALE KUNSTAUSSTELLUNG AUSSTELLUNG VON EINZELWERKEN DER BAUHAUSANGEHÖRIGEN. MALEREI UND PLASTIK IN RÄUMLICHER BINDUNG |
| **DIE BÜHNE** | zeigt Schau-Spiele, Spiele zum Schauen verschiedener Art, in denen die Ursprünge theatralischer Kunst zum Ausdruck kommen und zu neuen Wegen der Gestaltung führen. Sie sollen einer neuen Festlichkeit zum Siege helfen, die das Leben durchdringt. Die Bühnenkunst gleich der Architektur eine synthetische Kunst ist als Welt des Spiels und des Scheins Zufluchtsort des Irrationalen. | AUFFÜHRUNGEN DER BAUHAUSWOCHE AUSSTELLUNG VON ENTWÜRFEN, MODELLEN, FIGURINEN |

## DIE BAUHAUSWOCHE

bringt Vorträge über Bauhausbestrebungen, über Architektur, Kunst, Handwerk, Technik, Industrie, Schule, Erziehung; Aufführungen der Bühnenwerkstatt, Spielgänge, Tänze, Marionetten- u. Lichtspiele, Kino; Musikalische Veranstaltungen; ein Fest der Bauhäusler im Park von Weimar oder Umgebung

DEM STAATLICHEN BAUHAUS IN WEIMAR
SCHENKTEN DIESE WERKE

L, FEININGER / JOHANNES ITTEN
PAUL KLEE / GERHARD MARCKS
GEORG MUCHE / OSKAR SCHLEMMER
LOTHAR SCHREYER

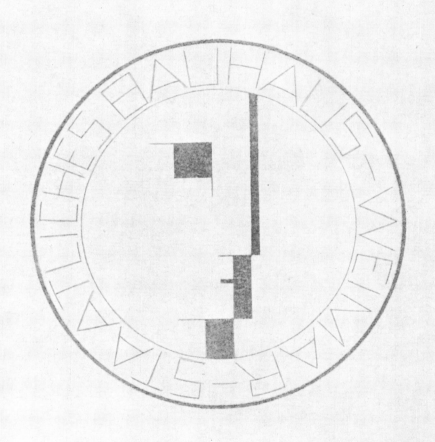

DIESE MAPPE TRÄGT DIE NUMMER   83

Lyonel Feininger and Oskar Schlemmer. Imprint of Bauhaus folder I *(10)*

IN DIESEM HAUSE GAB SICH
DAS DEUTSCHE VOLK DURCH
SEINE NATIONALVERSAMMLUNG
DIE WEIMARER VERFASSUNG
VOM 11. AUGUST 1919

Walter Gropius. Plaque on the Nationaltheater Weimar *(12)*

Laszlo Moholy-Nagy. Cover of "Idee und Aufbau des Staatlichen Bauhauses Weimar" by Walter Gropius (14)

Herbert Bayer. Binding: "Staatliches Bauhaus in Weimar 1919–1923" *(15)*

Lyonel Feininger and Paul Klee. Binding: Bauhaus folder I *(11)*

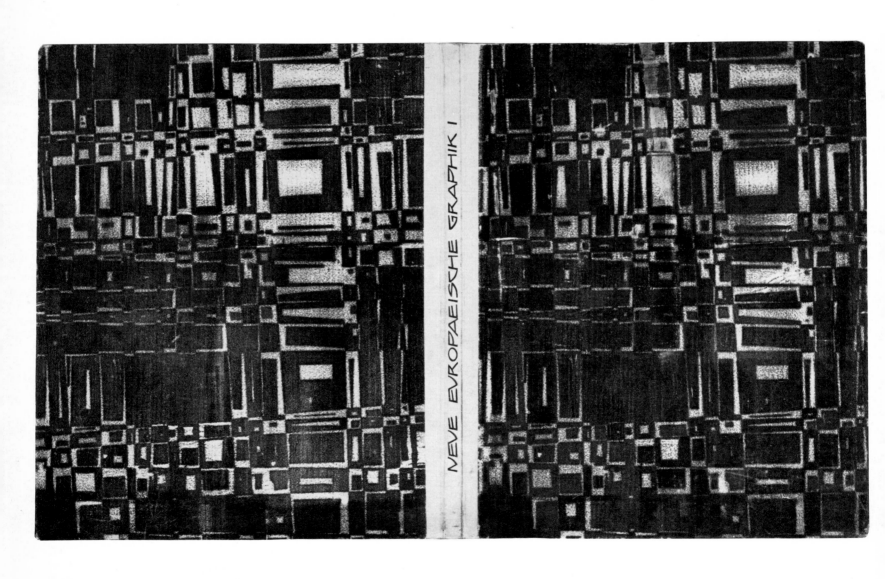

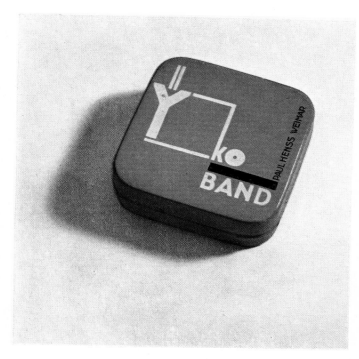

Joost Schmidt. Typewriter ribbon box *(17)*

Herbert Bayer. Bank-notes for the "land" Thuringia *(16)*

K. J. Jucker and
Wilhelm Wagen-
feld. Electric
table lamp *(42)*

Helene Jungnick. Large
divan cover with stripes (44)

Paul Klee (design). Tapestry with flying bird. Execution? (45)

Wilhelm Wagenfeld. Coffee and tea service (41)

Wilhelm Wagenfeld. Sauce-boat
with separate spouts for fat
and skim, and tray (40)

Helene Jungnick. Tapestry
(43)

Theo Bogler. Lidded dual
pot *(71)*

Benita Otte. Carpet for a nursery (46)

Unknown. Fabric
(58)

Theo Bogler.
Lidded pitcher (63)

Otto Lindig. Globular cocoa pot (77)

Suse Ackermann. Cover (49)

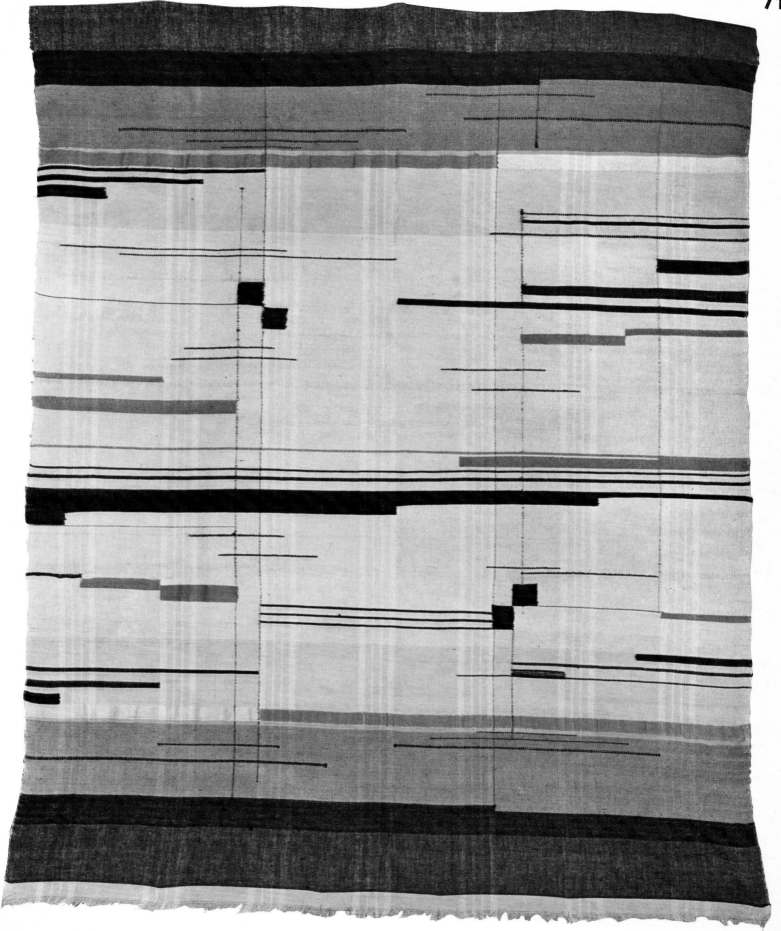

Gunta Stölzl.
Large cover (52)

Wilhelm Wagenfeld. Coffee pot *(37)*    W. Rössger and Friedrich Marby. Jug *(36)*

W. Rössger and Friedrich Marby.
Jug (36)

Wilhelm Wagenfeld.
Coffee pot (37)

Gunta Stölzl. Cover or runner *(51)*

Marianne Brandt.
Tea infuser
Julius Pap.
Liqueur bottle *(32)*

Marianne Brandt. Tea pot (34)

Otto Lindig. Tall flask *(89)*

Gunta Stölzl. Tapestry or cover *(50)*

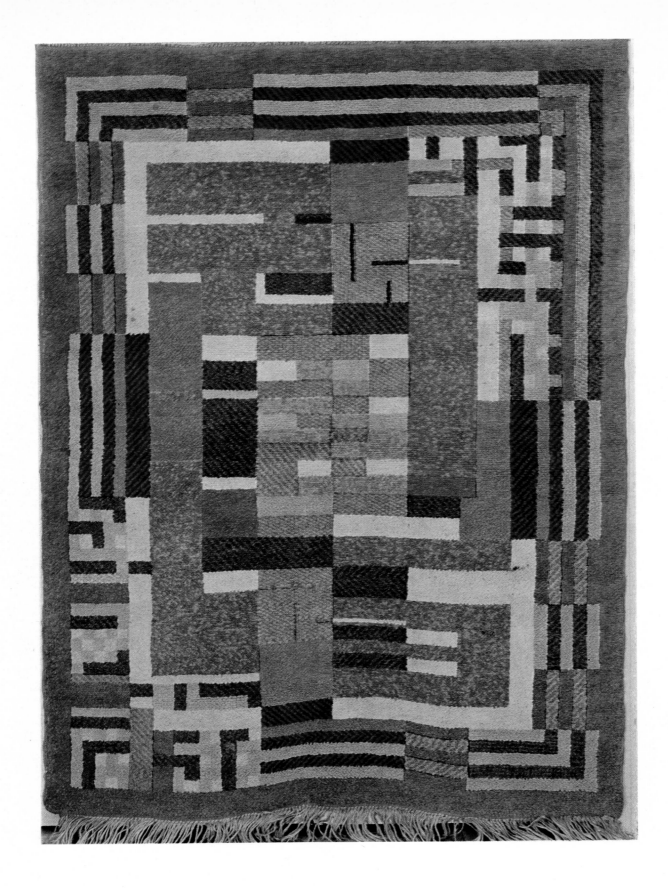

Benita Otte. Small carpet (47)

Wilhelm Wagenfeld. Tea caddy
Otto Rittweger and Wolfgang Tümpel. Stand with two infusing "spoons" (39)

Wilhelm Wagenfeld and
Wolfgang Tümpel.
Tea infusing "spoon"
and bowl (38)

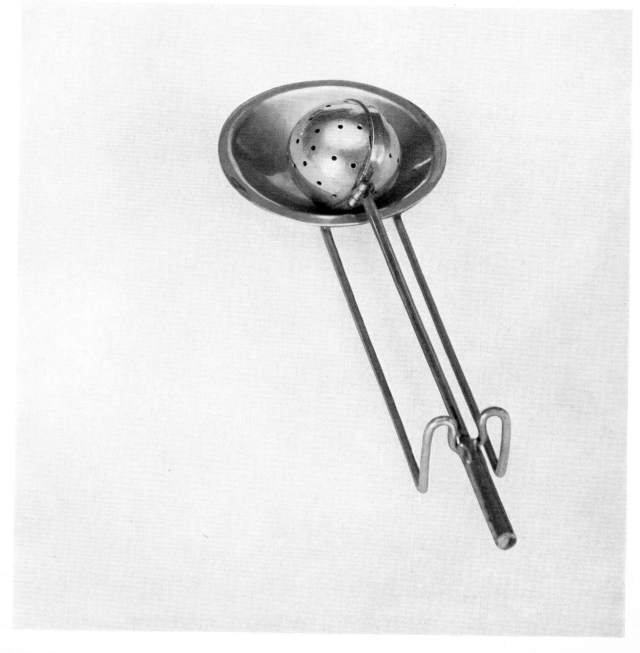

Marianne Heymann. Cushion cover *(55)*

Lies Beyer. Small
square cover *(53)*

Unknown. Coffee pot *(31)*

Marianne Brandt.
Tea infuser *(33)*

Otto Lindig.
Large dual pot (62)

Otto Lindig. Tea pot with strainer inside (75)

Otto Lindig. Lidded pitcher (67)

Gerhard Marcks and Theo Bogler.
Dual pot *(60)*

Gerhard Marcks and Otto Lindig.
Lidded jug (61)

Otto Lindig.
Water pitcher (65)

Otto Lindig. Lidded pitcher (69)

Theo Bogler. Dual pitcher (73)

Korona Krause. Cushion cover
(56)

Unknown. Water pitcher *(88)*

Theo Bogler. Lidded pot *(72)*

Theo Bogler. Tea pot with handle *(80)*

Agnes Roghé. Fabric *(57)*

Otto Lindig. Lidded jar
*(79)*

Gerhard Marcks. Tile for a stove in the "Töpferhaus" in Dornburg *(82)*

Gerhard Marcks and Max Krehan. Pitcher *(59)*

Theo Bogler.
Lidded pot (74)

Martin Jahn(?). Bulgy jug
with lid and spout *(30)*

Theo Bogler. Small tea urn
in four parts *(83)*

Otto Lindig.
Lidded pitcher (70)

Otto Lindig.
Lidded storage jar *(90)*

Otto Lindig.
Cup and milk jug (91)

Theo Bogler. Lidded pitcher (85)

Otto Lindig. Lidded
cocoa pot (84)

Marguerite Friedländer. Small mugs *(87)*

Otto Lindig. Cocoa pot (76)

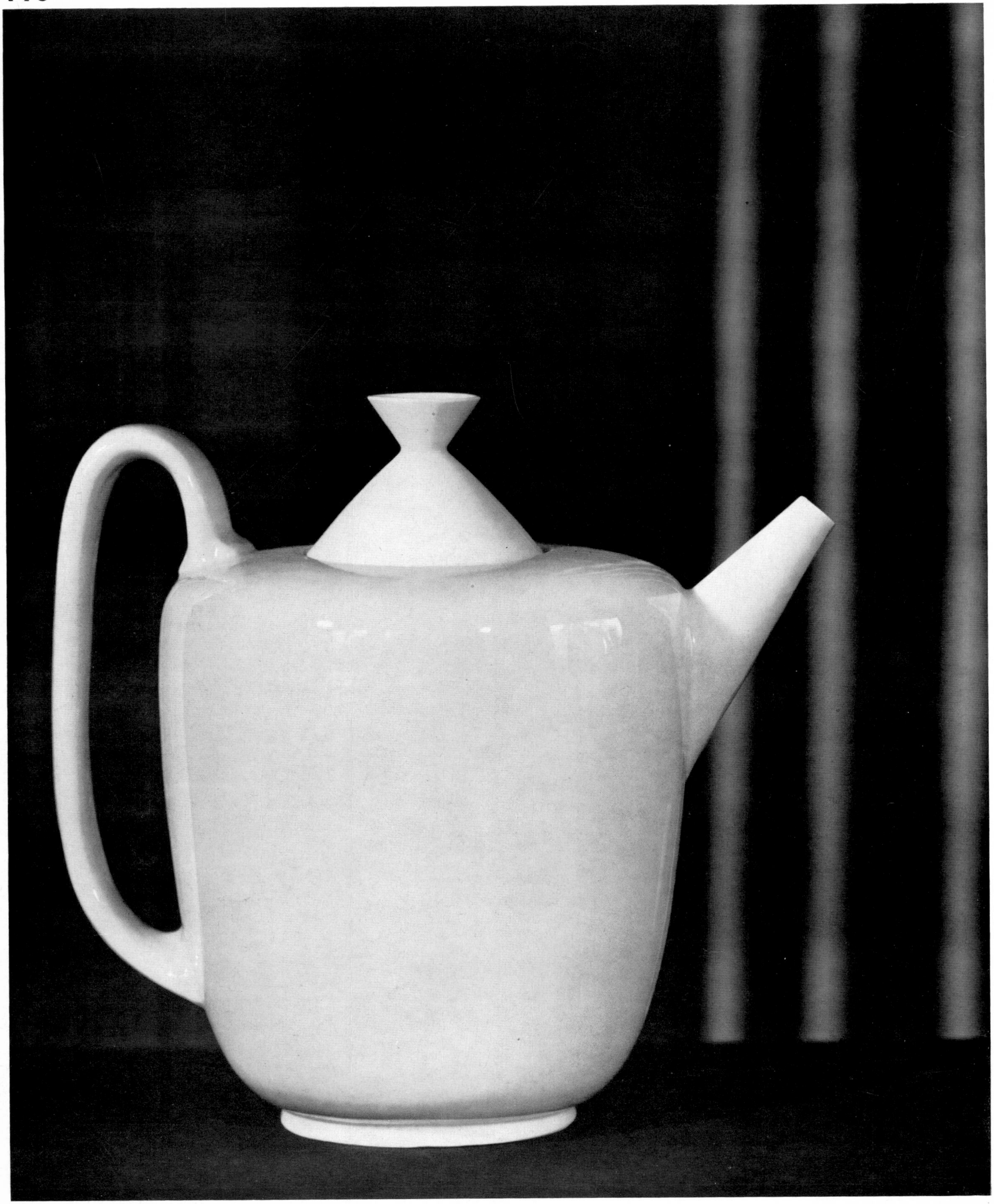

Otto Lindig. Coffee pot *(92)*

Marguerite Friedländer. Milk jug *(86)*

Otto Lindig.
Lidded jar (78)

Mila Hoffmann-Lederer. Shawl *(48)*

Otto Lindig. Beer jug
without lid (64)

Unknown. Small tapestry (54)

Theo Bogler. Lidded storage jar (81)

Marianne Brandt. Ashtray with tilting top (35)

Marcel Breuer and
Gunta Stölzl.
Chair with coloured
wool straps *(19)*

Erich Dickmann.
Upholstered
easy chair *(26)*

Marcel Breuer. Easy chair *(21)*

Marcel Breuer. Low tea table *(20)*

Marcel Breuer. Dining table *(23)*

Bengt von Rosen. Secretaire *(24)*

Marcel Breuer. Nursery table and chairs *(22)*

Erich Dickmann. Kitchen chair *(29)*

Josef Hartwig.
Bauhaus
chess men (25)

# LIST OF PLATES

## TYPOGRAPHY

**1 [42]** *Peter Röhl:* Publicity leaflet for the *Bauhaus-Abende*, 1920. Single folder. Lino-cut or line etching, black on white. 22.8 cm. × 14.6 cm.

**2 [43]** *Friedl Dicker:* Programme for the first *Bauhaus-Abend*, 14. 4. 1920. *Else Lasker-Schüler, eigene Dichtungen.* Single sheet, printed on both sides. Lithograph, black on white. 30.4 cm. × 24.7 cm.

**3 [41]** *Unknown:* Cover of *Nachrichtenblatt des Reichsbundes deutscher Kunsthochschüler*, No. I, 1 October 1920. Lithograph, black on reddish-brown. 29.2 cm. × 46.6 cm.

**4 [46]** *Unknown:* Programme of the *Richtfest* (workman's treat on setting up the roof of a new house) *Haus Sommerfeld, Berlin*, 18. 12. 1920. Single sheet, printed on both sides. Lithograph on hand-made paper, black on white. 78.2 cm. × 25.8 cm.

**5 [47]** *Farkas Molnar and H. Stefan:* Title-page of the folder *Italia*, with six lithographs by Molnar and six by Stefan, signed and dated 1922. Lithograph on hand-made paper. No. I blue and green on white, Ns. II–VI and VII–XII black on white. 44 cm. × 33.9 cm. (In folder, without imprint, 45.4 cm. × 35 cm.)

**6 [44]** *Johannes Itten and Friedl Dicker:* Text page from the yearbook *Utopia*, Weimar 1921, p. 29. Johannes Itten: *Analysen alter Meister.* Type and printing directed by Friedl Dicker. Letterpress and lithography. 32.6 cm. × 24.2 cm.

**7 [48]** *Oskar Schlemmer:* Cover of the yearbook *Utopia*, Weimar 1921, special edition. Lithograph, black on parchment paper, hand-coloured in gold, silver, red, orange, yellow, blue, violet and white. 32.8 cm. × 24.8 cm.

**8 [45]** *Johannes Itten:* Spruch (*Bauhaus* folder I/3), 1922/23, signed. Lithograph, blue, yellow, red, green, black on white. 34.9 cm. × 24.9 cm. (*Peters: Die Bauhaus-Mappen*, p. 24)

**9 [49]** *Lyonel Feininger:* Title-page: *Bauhaus* folder I, 1922/23, not signed. Lithograph, black on white. 55.8 cm. × 45 cm. (*Peters: Die Bauhaus-Mappen*, p. 19)

**10 [52]** *Lyonel Feininger and Oskar Schlemmer:* Imprint of *Bauhaus* folder I, 1922/23, not signed. Lettering by Feininger, lithograph, black on white. Imprint by Schlemmer, lithograph, pale ochre on white; number handwritten. 56 cm. × 45 cm. (*Peters: Die Bauhaus-Mappen*, p. 21)

**11 [56]** *Lyonel Feininger and Paul Klee:* Binding: *Bauhaus* folder I. Lettering by Feininger. Binding paper designed by Klee. Lithograph, black on parchment (spine) and black on white or pale blue paper (cover). 56 cm. × 90 cm. (*Peters: Die Bauhaus-Mappen*, p. 9.) The subscription prospectus states that prints were hand-produced in the printing workshop of the *Staatliches Bauhaus* (artistic director Lyonel Feininger, technical director Karl Zaubitzer). Binding from the bookbindery (artistic director Paul Klee, technical director Otto Dorfner).

**12 [53]** *Walter Gropius:* Plaque on the *Nationaltheater Weimar*, commemorating the Weimar Constitution of the German Republic. Unveiled 11 August 1922. Bronze cast. 75 cm. × 175 cm.

**13 [50]** *Oskar Schlemmer:* Publicity leaflet for the 1923 exhibition, unsigned. Double sheet, printed on both sides.
**[51]** Lithography and letterpress printing in yellow, blue, red, and black on white. (Printed by G. Christmann Nachf., Stuttgart.) 20.2 cm. × 30.2 cm. per double sheet. Text by Oskar Schlemmer, withdrawn before publication because of the expression "Cathedral of Socialism".

**14 [54]** *Laszlo Moholy-Nagy:* Cover of *Idee und Aufbau des Staatlichen Bauhauses Weimar* by Walter Gropius. *Bauhaus-Verlag München GmbH*, 1923. Offprint from *Staatliches Bauhaus in Weimar 1919–1923* with new paging. Letterpress black on yellow by F. Bruckmann AG, Munich. 25 cm. × 25 cm.

**15 [55]** *Herbert Bayer:* Binding: *Staatliches Bauhaus in Weimar 1919–1923. Bauhaus-Verlag* Weimar/Munich, 1923. Lithography, red and blue on black. Binding by Dietsch & Brückner, Weimar. 24.7 cm. × 24.7 cm.

**16 [57]** *Herbert Bayer:* Bank-notes for the "land" Thuringia. Two million and one million marks, issued 9 August 1923. Letterpress and lithography on white with underprint violet, blue, green, and ochre. 7.3 cm. × 14.3 cm.

**17 [57]** *Joost Schmidt:* Typewriter ribbon box. Messrs. Paul Henss, Weimar, 1924/25. Tin box, letters black and white on tomato red. 5.6 cm. × 5.6 cm. × 1.9 cm. (Part of the firm's uniform publicity, designed by Joost Schmidt.)

## CABINET-MAKING AND WOOD-CARVING

**18 [124]** *Peter Keler:* Cradle, 1922. Open sides filled with raffia. Colours after Kandinsky's colour theory: end boards yellow, side panels red, hoop rockers blue. Painted wood. 98 cm. × 91.7 cm. × 91.7 cm. Restored in 1964 from instructions given by Peter Keler. (*Bauhaus 1919–1923*, p. 79)

**19 [125]** *Marcel Breuer and Gunta Stölzl:* Chair by Breuer. Coloured wool straps, woven by Stölzl, 1922/23. Pear, polished black. Height 75.5 cm., width 49 cm., depth 49 cm. (*Bauhaus 1919–1923*, p. 81)

**20 [130]** *Marcel Breuer:* Low tea table, 1921/22. Pear, polished black, round, on five angular legs. Diameter of the table-top 111 cm., legs 56 cm., height of the table-top 44 cm. (*Bauhaus 1919–1923*, p. 74)

**21 [128]** *Marcel Breuer:* Easy chair, 1922. Frame: polished cherry. Straps and seat material: rusty brown. Height
**[129]** 96 cm., width 56 cm., depth 57 cm. (*Bauhaus 1919–1923*, p. 83)

**22 [133]** *Marcel Breuer:* Nursery table and chairs, 1923. Planed wood and sheets of plywood, painted in oils. Chair frames: red; seats: white; table: grey and white. Table: height 50 cm., width 49.5 cm., depth 49.5 cm. Chairs: height 59 cm., width 26.5 cm., depth 32 cm. (*Neue Arbeiten*, p. 32 and colour plate.)

**23 [131]** *Marcel Breuer:* Dining table, 1924. Natural cherry, stained. Rectangular legs, transposed. Height 73 cm., width 95 cm., depth 95 cm. (*Neue Arbeiten*, p. 22)

**24 [132]** *Bengt von Rosen:* Secretaire, 1923/24. Reddish cherry and dark brown plum. Outside: natural; inside: stained greenish. Height 128 cm., width 82 cm., depth 44 cm. (*Neue Arbeiten*, p. 13)

**25 [136]** *Josef Hartwig:* Bauhaus chess men, 1923/24. 32 pieces, signed "Hartwig Bauhaus Weimar Ges. Gesch.". Natural pear, stained black. Cloth bases. Box brown beech. Pawn 22 × 22 × 22 mm. Castle 37 × 27 × 27 mm. Queen 50 × 27 × 27 mm. King 55 × 27 × 27 mm. From the left to the right: above: king, queen, castle; below: knight, bishop, pawn. (*Neue Arbeiten*, p. 43–45, variants.)

**26 [127]** *Erich Dickmann:* Upholstered easy chair, 1924. Walnut; dark brown upholstery. Height 72 cm., width 62 cm., depth 82 cm. (Originally owned by the master cabinet-maker, Weidensee, *Bauhaus*.)

**27 [126]** *Erich Dickmann:* Writing desk, 1924. Two doors each side. Polished walnut. Height 72 cm., width 138.5 cm., depth 72 cm. (Originally owned by the master cabinet-maker, Weidensee, *Bauhaus*.)

**28 [134]** *Erich Dickmann:* Easy chair, cane back and seat for loose cushions, 1924. Beech, brown stained. Height 81 cm., width 62 cm., depth 73 cm. (*Staatliche Bauhochschule Weimar*, prospectus 1927, p. 33)

**29 [135]** *Erich Dickmann:* Kitchen chair. Natural beech. Seat and back cream-coloured body varnish. Height 80 cm., width 43 cm., depth 43 cm. (Originally owned by the master cabinet-maker, Weidensee, *Bauhaus*.)

## METALWORK

**30 [107]** *Martin Jahn*(?): Bulgy jug with lid and spout, 1921/22. Copper, embossed and rivetted. Ebony fitting. Silver plated inside. Height 19.5 cm.

**31 [88]** *Unknown:* Coffee pot, 1921/22. German silver, embossed. Ebony fittings. Height 18.5 cm.

**32 [78]** *Marianne Brandt:* Tea infuser, 1923/24. Bronze, ebony handle, silver mounts. Silver plated inside. Height 12.5 cm.
*Julius Pap:* Liqueur bottle, 1922. Body: bronze; the rest: German silver. Height 33 cm. (*Bauhaus 1919–1923,* plate 107)

**33 [89]** *Marianne Brandt:* Tea infuser, 1924. Bronze, ebony handles, silver mounts. Silver plated inside. Height 7.8 cm. (*Neue Arbeiten,* p. 46)

**34 [79]** *Marianne Brandt:* Tea pot, 1924. Service contains cream jug, sugar bowl and tray. Brass, with ebony handles and German silver mounts. Silver plated inside. Height 17.5 cm. (*Neue Arbeiten,* pp. 48/49, variant.)

**35 [123]** *Marianne Brandt:* Ashtray with tilting top, 1924. Bronze, German silver top. Height 5.5 cm.

**36 [74]** *W. Rössger and Friedrich Marby:* Jug, 1923/24. German silver and tombac. Height 19 cm. (*Neue Arbeiten,* p. 58)

**37 [75]** *Wilhelm Wagenfeld:* Coffee pot, 1923/24. German silver. *Bauhaus* hall-mark. Height 19 cm. (*Bauhaus 1919–1923,* plate 112)

**[73]** See: Nos. 36, 37

**38 [85]** *Wilhelm Wagenfeld and Wolfgang Tümpel:* Tea infusing "spoon" (Tümpel) and bowl (Wagenfeld), 1924. German silver. Bowl: diameter 5.8 cm. "Spoon" with handle: length 15.3 cm. (*Neue Arbeiten,* p. 63)

**39 [84]** *Wilhelm Wagenfeld:* Tea caddy, 1924. German silver. Height 14.9 cm. (*Neue Arbeiten,* p. 62)
*Otto Rittweger and Wolfgang Tümpel:* Stand (Rittweger) with two infusing "spoons" (Tümpel), 1924. German silver. Stand: height 20 cm., diameter 10.5 cm. "Spoon" with handle: length 15.3 cm. (*Neue Arbeiten,* p. 61)

**40 [63]** *Wilhelm Wagenfeld:* Sauce-boat, with separate spouts for fat and skim, and tray, 1924. German silver, ebony handles. Height 15.2 cm. Tray: diameter 15.2 cm. *Bauhaus* hall-mark. (*Neue Arbeiten,* p. 54, variant.)

**41 [62]** *Wilhelm Wagenfeld:* Coffee and tea service, 1924. German silver with ebony mounts. *Bauhaus* hall-mark on tray. Coffee pot: height 22.5 cm. Tea pot: height 14 cm. Milk jug: height 12 cm. Tray: diameter 39 × 26.5 cm. (*Neue Arbeiten*, p. 56, with sugar bowl, not shown here.)

**42 [58]** *K. J. Jucker and Wilhelm Wagenfeld:* Electric table lamp, 1923/24. Glass stand and tube, opalescent glass shade. Brass and German silver mounts. Height 39 cm. (*Neue Arbeiten*, p. 68)

## WEAVING

**43 [64]** *Helene Jungnick:* Tapestry, abstract design, 1921/22. Warp knotted into fringe, different materials in dark colours. 90 cm. × 125 cm. (*Bauhaus 1919–1923*, p. 134, ill. 88)

**44 [59]** *Helene Jungnick:* Large divan cover with stripes, 1922/23. Warp knotted into fringe, wool, cotton, and artificial silk, black and white. 164 cm. × 249 cm.

**45 [60]** *Paul Klee:* Design; execution? Tapestry with flying bird. Warp knotted into fringe, wool, red, yellow,
**[61]** brown, blue, and white. 142 cm. × 285 cm. Attributed to Paul Klee by Margarete Koehler-Bittkow, apprentice in the *Bauhaus* weaving workshop from 1919–1923

**46 [66]** *Benita Otte:* Carpet for a nursery, 1923. White warp, beige, grey, blue, yellow, light-red, turquoise-green
**[67]** woof. Warp knotted into fringe. Cotton. 177 cm. × 101 cm. (*Neue Arbeiten*, colour plate opposite p. 32)

**47 [82]** *Benita Otte:* Small carpet, 1923. Knotted carpet on grey warp, violet, grey-green, blue-grey, yellow-green,
**[83]** green, strawberry-pink, and cardinal red woof. Wool. 205 cm. × 152 cm.

**48 [119]** *Mila Hoffmann-Lederer:* Shawl, 1923/24. On a white warp, arrow shapes in wool, the rest fine silk, hemmed. 250 cm. × 75 cm.

**49 [71]** *Suse Ackermann:* Cover, 1923/24. On white and salmon-pink warp, with woof in black, white, grey, orange, yellow, and others. Warp knotted into fringe. Wool and cotton. 140 cm. × 109 cm.

**50 [81]** *Gunta Stölzl:* Tapestry or cover, 1923/24. Warp white with a few black threads, woof grey, black, and natural wool, with a few stripes of gold-coloured metal thread. Sheep's wool and artificial silk, hemmed. 182 cm. × 119 cm.

**51 [76]** *Gunta Stölzl:* Cover or runner, 1923. Flat weaving, with turned shuttles. Black, white, brown, grey, and
**[77]** violet. Wool and viscose silk. 241 cm. × 102 cm. (*Neue Arbeiten*, ill. 86)

**52 [72]** *Gunta Stölzl:* Large cover, 1923. White warp, alternating between wool and artificial silk. White woof, with several shades of grey. Leaf-weaving, in wool and artificial silk. Long knotted fringe on all four edges. 185 cm. × 167 cm. (*Neue Arbeiten*, ill. 87)

**53 [87]** *Lies Beyer:* Small square cover, 1923/24. Twill-weaving on rusty red warp, white, olive, blue, grey, brown, and yellow. Linen, hemmed. 105 cm. × 105 cm.

**54 [121]** *Unknown:* Small tapestry, 1922/23. Black, white, grey, and orange stripes on black warp. Wool, artificial silk, and mixed thread, hemmed. 142 cm. × 125 cm.

**55 [86]** *Marianne Heymann:* Cushion cover, 1923/24. Orange-red warp, woof blue, red, violet, orange, green, white, and shades of these. Cotton, wool, artificial silk, hemmed. 78 cm. × 106 cm.

**56 [98]** *Korona Krause:* Cushion cover, 1923/24. Warp in shades of red, woof in stripes of green, purple, orange, black, white, and shades of these. Cotton and artificial silk. Warp ending in fringe. 66 cm. × 120 cm.

**57 [102]** *Agnes Roghé:* Fabric, 1923/24. Linsey-woolsey, with transposed squares in black, white, blue, yellow, and red. Woven on Jacquard loom? 280 cm. × 95 cm.

**58 [68]** *Unknown:* Fabric, 1923/24. White warp, woof in stripes of black, white, yellow, and pink. Cotton, synthetic wool, and artificial silk. 125 cm. × 78 cm.


## POTTERY

**59 [105]** *Gerhard Marcks and Max Krehan:* Pitcher, 1921/22. Pale ochre earthenware, thrown. Décor dark brown, dark green, and blue. Cubist design of fishes. Pitcher by Krehan, décor by Marcks. Scratched signature by Marcks ⚹. Height 39.5 cm. (*Janda*, No. 1)

**60 [92]** *Gerhard Marcks and Theo Bogler:* Dual pot, 1921. Grey-yellow earthenware, iron-grey mat finish, lighter at the edges. Pot by Bogler, décor by Marcks. Scratched signature by Bogler ⚲ and Marcks ⚹. Height – with lid – 34 cm. (*Janda*, No. 47)

**61 [93]** *Gerhard Marcks and Otto Lindig:* Lidded jug, 1922. Pale reddish earthenware, thrown. Décor brown and dark green, translucent finish. Jug by Lindig, décor by Marcks(?). Scratched signature by Lindig ⚲. Height – with lid – 27 cm. (*Janda*, No. 10)

**62 [90]** *Otto Lindig:* Large dual pot, 1922. Reddish-yellow earthenware, thrown. Iron-grey mat finish, stripes sparred out. Greenish inside. China-ink signature by Lindig ♀. Height – with lid – 31 cm. (*Janda*, No. 9)

**63 [69]** *Theo Bogler:* Lidded pitcher, 1921/22. Pale yellow-pink earthenware, thrown. Medium brown lustre glazing outside. Pale olive-green finish inside. Scratched signature by Bogler ⚡. Height – with lid – 28.7 cm. (*Janda*, No. 48)

**64 [120]** *Otto Lindig:* Beer jug without lid, 1922. Pale yellow earthenware, thrown. Golden brown finish. Scratched signature by Lindig ♀. Height 33 cm. (*Bauhaus 1919–1923*, p. 123, variant; *Janda*, No. 12)

**65 [95]** *Otto Lindig:* Water pitcher, 1922. Greyish-yellow earthenware, thrown. Yellow-brown finish outside. Scratched signature by Lindig ♀. Height 55 cm. (*Janda*, No. 3)

**66 [94]** *Otto Lindig:* Globular water pitcher, 1922. Pale yellow earthenware, thrown. Dark brown finish outside, greyish-green inside. Scratched signature by Lindig ♀. Height 43 cm. (*Janda*, No. 6)

**67 [91]** *Otto Lindig:* Lidded pitcher, 1921/22. Greyish-brown earthenware, thrown. Blackish-brown high glaze. Scratched signature by Lindig ♀. Height – with lid – 51.5 cm. (*Janda*, No. 5)

**68 [114]** *Otto Lindig:* Lidded beer jug, August 1922. Pale yellow earthenware, thrown. Yellow high glaze. Scratched signature by Lindig ♀ with addition "VIII 22". Height – with lid – 51 cm. (*Janda*, No. 7)

**69 [96]** *Otto Lindig:* Lidded pitcher, 1922. Pale yellow earthenware, thrown. Gold flecked brown finish. Scratched signature by Lindig ♀. Height – with lid – 48 cm. (*Janda*, No. 13)

**70 [108]** *Otto Lindig:* Lidded pitcher, 1922/23. Whitish earthenware, thrown. Cream finish with few purple dashes. Base mounted on German silver (hiding a flaw?). Scratched signature by Lindig ♀. Height – with lid – 43 cm. (*Janda*, No. 11)

**71 [65]** *Theo Bogler:* Lidded dual pot, 1922. Yellowish-grey earthenware, thrown. Outside: top brownish, below dark olive finish. All inside: pale olive. Scratched signature by Bogler ℔. Height – with lid – 32.5 cm. (*Janda*, No. 54)

**72 [100]** *Theo Bogler:* Lidded pot, 1922/23. Pale yellowish-red earthenware, thrown. Outside: top dark brown, base light brown finish. All inside: greenish. Scratched signature by Bogler ℔. Height – with handle – 23 cm. (*Janda*, No. 58)

**73 [97]** *Theo Bogler:* Dual pitcher, 1922. Pale yellow earthenware, thrown. Whitish-grey finish. Scratched signature by Bogler ℔. Height 23 cm. (*Janda*, No. 59)

**74 [106]** *Theo Bogler:* Lidded pot, 1922/23. Yellowish-red earthenware, thrown. Golden brown finish outside. Chrome yellow inside. Scratched signature by Bogler ᛒ. Height 29 cm. (*Janda*, No. 53)

**75 [91]** *Otto Lindig:* Tea pot with strainer inside, 1922/23. Brick-red earthenware, thrown. Part of outside iron-grey mat finish. Scratched signature by Lindig � . Height – with lid – 18.5 cm. (*Janda*, No. 22)

**76 [115]** *Otto Lindig:* Cocoa pot, 1923. Reddish-brown earthenware, moulded. Pale grey translucent finish. Unsigned. Height – with lid – 15.7 cm. (*Neue Arbeiten*, p. 94; *Janda*, No. 36)

**77 [70]** *Otto Lindig:* Globular cocoa pot, 1923. Yellowish earthenware, moulded. Brown finish, with parts sparred out on lid. Scratched signature by Lindig ☿. Height – with lid – 17.5 cm. (*Neue Arbeiten*, p. 94; *Janda*, No. 37)

**78 [118]** *Otto Lindig:* Lidded jar (the "classic" Lindig shape), 1924. Ochre earthenware, moulded. Pale grey finish with dark brown stripes. Unsigned. Height – with lid – 29.5 cm. (*Neue Arbeiten*, p. 100; *Janda*, No. 30)

**79 [103]** *Otto Lindig:* Lidded jar, 1924. Reddish-brown earthenware, moulded. Pale grey translucent finish. Unsigned. Height – with lid – 16 cm. (*Janda*, No. 40)

**80 [101]** *Theo Bogler:* Tea pot with handle, 1922/23. Dark red earthenware, moulded. Iron-grey mat finish. Metal handle raffia-covered. Unsigned. Height – without handle – 11.8 cm. (*Bauhaus 1919–1923*, p. 127; *Neue Arbeiten*, p. 102/3; *Janda*, No. 69)

**81 [122]** *Theo Bogler:* Lidded storage jar, 1923. Reddish-brown earthenware, moulded. Pale grey translucent finish. Unsigned. Height – with lid – 17.5 cm. (*Neue Arbeiten*, p. 105; *Janda*, No. 60)

**82 [104]** *Gerhard Marcks:* Tile for a stove in the *Töpferhaus* in Dornburg, 1921. Pale grey earthenware with markings and grey-brown slip. Unglazed. 18.5 cm. × 18.5 cm.

**83 [107]** *Theo Bogler:* Small tea urn, in four parts: lidded tea pot, tea strainer, ring, brazier. 1923. Pale yellow earthenware, moulded. Outside: mat and high glaze black finish, rims unglazed. Inside: golden yellow. Scratched signature and date (1923) by Bogler ᛒ. All-over height 25.5 cm. (tea pot – with lid – 13 cm., ring 6.3 cm., base 10.5 cm.). (*Neue Arbeiten*, p. 109; *Bauhaus 1919–1923*, p. 125; *Janda*, No. 50)

**84 [112]** *Otto Lindig:* Lidded cocoa pot, 1923. Dark red earthenware, moulded. Brown and grey finish. Unsigned. Height – with lid – 23.7 cm. (*Neue Arbeiten*, p. 107; *Janda*, No. 31)

**85 [111]** *Theo Bogler:* Lidded pitcher, 1923/24. Natural clay earthenware, thrown. Coffee-coloured high glaze. Scratched signature by Bogler ᛒ, and *Bauhaus* mark. Height – with lid – 34.5 cm. (*Janda*, No. 56)

**86 [117]** *Marguerite Friedländer:* Milk jug, 1923. Pale yellow earthenware, moulded. Yellow crackle glazing. Scratched signature by Friedländer 禾. Height 13.2 cm. (*Janda*, No. 80)

**87 [113]** *Marguerite Friedländer:* Small mugs, 1923. Ochre earthenware, moulded. Different finishes. Scratched signature by Friedländer 禾. Height 9.8 cm. (*Neue Arbeiten*, p. 108; *Janda*, No. 77/79)

**88 [99]** *Unknown:* Water pitcher, 1923. Pale grey earthenware, thrown. Cobalt-blue deckle and salt glaze (*Blaue Schürze*). Unsigned. Height 21 cm. (*Janda*, No. 84)

**89 [80]** *Otto Lindig:* Tall flask, 1922/23. Pale grey earthenware, thrown. Cobalt-blue deckle and salt glaze (*Blaue Schürze*). China-ink signature by Lindig ♀. Height 41.5 cm. (*Janda*, No. 15)

**90 [109]** *Otto Lindig:* Lidded storage jar, 1923/24. Pale yellow-red earthenware, thrown. Outside mat black finish, greenish-yellow inside. Scratched signature by Lindig ♀, and label with *Bauhaus* mark. Height – with lid – 27.5 cm. (*Janda*, No. 21)

**91 [110]** *Otto Lindig:* Cup and milk jug, 1924. Yellowish-red earthenware, moulded. Outside dark grey finish, inside pale olive. Unsigned. Cup: height 5.5 cm.; saucer: diameter 14.4 cm.; milk jug: height 11.5 cm. (*Janda*, No. 41)

**92 [116]** *Otto Lindig:* Coffee pot, 1923. White porcelain, from model by Lindig. *Staatliche Manufaktur Berlin.* Unsigned, label with *Bauhaus* mark. Height – with lid – 18 cm. (*Janda*, No. 25)

# BIBLIOGRAPHY

**Adler,** Bruno, Das Weimarer Bauhaus, Darmstadt 1966

**Albers,** Joseph, Over mijn leven. Catalogue of the exhibition in the Stedelijk Museum, Amsterdam 1961

**Argan,** Giulio Carlo, Gropius und das Bauhaus, Hamburg 1962

**Banham,** Reyner, Theory and Design in the First Machine Age. Architectural Press, London 1960; F.A. Praeger Inc., New York 1960

**Bauhaus in Weimar,** Staatliches, 1919–1923, Weimar–Munich 1923

**Bayer,** Herbert, and **Gropius,** Ilse and Walter, Bauhaus 1919–1928, Museum of Modern Art, Boston 1938; Allen and Unwin, London 1939

**Belloli,** Carlo, Il contributo Russo alle avanguardie plastiche. Catalogo No. 11, Galleria del Levante, Milano 1964

**Deventer,** Salomon van, Henry van de Velde und seine Bindungen an das Ehepaar Kröller-Müller, privately printed 1963

**Erffa,** Helmut von, Bauhaus, First Phase, Architectural Review, August 1957, London 1957

**Gräff,** Werner, Catalogue of the exhibition of the Kunstverein Rheinland-Westfalen, Düsseldorf 1962

**Gropius,** Walter, Nachruf auf Adolf Meyer, "Das Neue Frankfurt". III. 1929, No. 9

**Gropius,** Walter, New Architecture and the Bauhaus, Faber and Faber, London 1935; W.I.T. Press, Massachusetts Institute of Technology, Cambridge, Mass.

**Gropius,** Walter, Scope of Total Architecture, Harper & Row, New York 1953; Allen & Unwin, London 1956

**Gropius,** Walter and **Moholy-Nagy,** Laszlo, Neue Arbeiten der Bauhaus-Werkstätten (Bauhaus-Bücher, Vol. VII), Munich 1925

**Hartwig,** Josef, Leben und Meinungen des Bildhauers Josef Hartwig, Frankfurt/Main 1955

**Hess,** Hans, Feininger, Abrams, New York 1961; Thames and Hudson, London 1961

**Hüter,** Karl Heinz, Van de Veldes Kunstgewerbeschule in Weimar, Zeitschrift der Hochschule für Architektur Weimar. IX. 1962, pp. 9ff. and 101 ff.

**Itten,** Johannes, Mein Vorkurs am Bauhaus, Ravensburg 1963

**Jaffe,** H. L. C., De Stijl, Amsterdam 1956

**Janda,** Annegret, Bauhaus-Keramik, Kunstmuseen der DDR, Mitteilungen, Vol. II, 1959, p. 83ff.

**Mahler-Werfel,** Alma, ...and the Bridge is Love, Harcourt, Brace and World, New York 1958

**Mehring,** Walter, Verrufene Malerei, Zurich 1958

**Moholy-Nagy,** Laszlo, Vom Material zur Architektur (Bauhaus-Bücher, Vol. XIV), Munich 1929

**Moholy-Nagy,** Sibyll, Laszlo Moholy-Nagy, Harper and Row, New York 1950

**Muche,** Georg, Blickpunkt Sturm, Dada, Bauhaus, Gegenwart, Munich 1961

**Pazitnov,** L., Das schöpferische Erbe des Bauhauses 1919–1933 (Studienreihe Angewandte Kunst, Neuzeit, No. 1), Berlin 1963

**Peters,** Heinz, Die Bauhaus-Mappen, Cologne 1957

**Pevsner,** Nicolaus, Academies of Past and Present, Cambridge 1940

**Pevsner,** Nicolaus, Pioneers of Modern Design, Doubleday, New York 1958; Penguin Books, London 1960

**Pevsner,** Nicolaus, Gropius and van de Velde, Architectural Review, March 1963, London 1963

**Pietschmann,** Karl, Mit Verstand und Herz, Schwerin 1954

**Richter,** Hans, Ein Leben für Bild und Film. Catalogue of the exhibition of the Akademie der Künste, Berlin 1958

**Scheidig,** Walther, Die Weimarer Malerschule. Exhibition catalogue, Weimar 1960

**Schenk zu Schweinsberg,** Eberhard Frh., Otto Lindig, Keramik, Berlin 1942

**Schlemmer,** Oskar, Briefe und Tagebücher, Munich 1958

**Schreyer,** Lothar, Erinnerungen an Sturm und Bauhaus, Munich 1956

**Stravinsky,** Igor, Autobiography, Gollancz, London 1936; Simon and Schuster, New York 1936

**Wingler,** Hans Maria, Das Bauhaus, Bramsche 1963

# INDEX OF NAMES

The number in Roman type is the number of the respective page.
The number in italics is the respective page-number of the List of Plates and of the plate.